We the People

Your Constitution in *Action*

by Pamela A. Marx, J.D.

Good Year Books

Parsippany, New Jersey

Acknowledgments

To Mark and to my parents

Many thanks and grateful acknowledgments go to Derek Steinorth,
his class at Eagle Rock Junior High School, Roberta Dempsey,
Suzanne Beason, Mary Wynton, Mark Goldstein, Megan Goldstein,
and Holly Goldstein.

Good Year Books

are available for most basic curriculum subjects plus many enrichment areas. For
more Good Year Books, contact your local bookseller or educational dealer. For a
complete catalog with information about other Good Year Books, please write:

Good Year Books
299 Jefferson Road
Parsippany, NJ 07054
www.pearsonlearning.com
1-800-321-3106

Cover and Interior Design: Anne Ricigliano
Design Manager: M. Jane Heelan
Editorial Manager: Suzanne Gaffney Beason
Executive Editor: Judith Adams

This Book Is Printed
On Recycled Paper

Table of Contents

Introduction

The purpose of this book is to help students in grades five and up to discover that the Constitution can speak to them directly—that is, they can read it and understand it—and to provoke thoughtful responses to the issues the Constitution has raised and continues to raise today. While not every section of the Constitution is covered in detail, an effort has been made to provide activities for those important sections that a maturing student can grasp.

Teachers may choose to use this book in its entirety or on a piecemeal basis. Because the text often directly relates provisions of the Constitution to historical events, a teacher may choose from among various activities in order to integrate the study of the Constitution into the general history curriculum.

The Constitution sets forth the rules by which the federal government operates and the relationship between the federal government and the government of each state. It begins with the Preamble, which is followed by Articles I through VII. Each Article includes a number of sections. In longer articles, such as those that describe the function of each branch of the federal government, the sections are divided into clauses. The twenty-seven Amendments to the Constitution follow Article VII. The first ten Amendments are often referred to as the Bill of Rights. The subject matter of this book follows the general order of the Constitution itself, except that Amendments to the Constitution are often discussed in the context of the Article sections they were adopted to modify.

Articles I through III—which describe the powers and duties of the three branches of our government—form a significant portion of the book. Discussion of these three articles and the first ten Amendments is probably the most valuable aspect of this book in terms of providing students with an understanding of democratic thought and governance.

How This Book Is Set Up

This book provides students with opportunities to read and evaluate provisions of the Constitution, engage in analytical thinking about constitutional issues, and investigate additional research resources. When considering the activities suggested, it is important to remember that this book is a teaching tool that offers young minds a starting place for thinking about constitutional issues. As such, this book does not discuss the issues raised by the Constitution in precisely the same way a lawyer or court would. This does not minimize the value of the discussion for raising general issues for student consideration.

Read-and-Answer/Take Another Look Most of this book is devoted to a series of two-page activity sheets. The left-hand page is called "Read-and-Answer." Here, the student is asked to read a portion of the Constitution and provide salient information from the text. Occasionally, there is a more open-ended or interpretive question on this page. The right-hand page is called "Take Another Look." Here the student is offered two or three activities for more in-depth exploration of the constitutional sections under review. For example, an activity may ask a student to explore a specific part of the Constitution, or may identify historical situations in which the constitutional provision was at issue and ask the student to investigate it. An activity may also cite Supreme Court cases in which the constitutional section was interpreted, and then ask for the student's viewpoint. Unless otherwise indicated, the activities on this page are intended as individual student endeavors. Activities geared for groups are identified as such.

The last activity on this page is identified as "Being a Citizen." This activity helps the student develop the skills of a thinking and active citizen. It may ask the student to seek out current information about different leaders today and their constitutional roles. It may provide an opportunity to debate an important issue. Analysis and discussion of issues is ever important to an active, vibrant democratic government.

The subject matter of many of the activities suggested in "Take Another Look" may require the teacher to introduce the assignment with some explanation and discussion. Such discussion should motivate students and enable them to participate in the analytical process.

You Be the Judge These are three individual activities that offer students opportunities to consider the relevance of certain liberties guaranteed in the Bill of Rights. These activities encourage students to analyze factual situations similar to those reviewed by the Supreme Court. Each activity begins with a description of the facts of the case. Students are then given arguments that each side might present in a court of law. The students then perform their own balancing test, weighing the rights of the individual against, for example, the interests of the government, to determine if any rights were violated. Students are invited to render decisions on the outcome of each case. Finally, they can compare their decisions with those of the Supreme Court. They have the opportunity to check whether their judgment in the case was similar to that of the nine justices.

These activities are designed to help students recognize that, as participants in a democratic society, each individual has rights and responsibilities. One individual's rights extend no further than another person's individual rights, and so rights must be exercised responsibly.

Guide to Cited Cases This section gives brief summary information about each of the Supreme Court cases cited in the activity pages. This background information may be useful to teachers and students in understanding the material.

Text of the Constitution The full text of the Constitution is included at the end of the book. It can be copied and given to students to keep in their notebooks. Those sections that have been modified by Amendment are italicized for easy identification.

Constitutional Resources—Books, the Internet, and Beyond This section provides a listing of constitutional materials, educational organizations, and Internet sites. Some of the books and Web sites may be useful resources for researching "Take Another Look" activities.

Answer Key This section provides answers to the questions from the "Read-and-Answer" pages.

The colonial leaders who wrote the Constitution were perhaps wiser than even they could have imagined. The governmental framework they designed has been flexible enough to adapt to the tremendous changes our country has undergone through the centuries. The Constitution has taken the United States from its infancy to a sprawling country of fifty diverse states. It has served the nation well as our population has grown and diversified, our technologies have been revolutionized, and world conditions have been drastically altered. The Constitution's simplicity has been fundamental to our nation's ability to meet the challenges of these changing conditions and will undoubtedly allow it to do so in the future. The more students know about the role the Constitution plays in their lives, the better prepared they will be as future voters and leaders. Being an educated citizen in a democratic country is a lifelong responsibility, and this book can provide a first step in that learning process.

Exploring the Constitution

The Preamble

The Constitution is a set of rules by which the United States is governed. It was written during the hot, muggy summer of 1787 by a group of men that included Benjamin Franklin, Alexander Hamilton, James Madison, and George Washington. There were many disagreements to be resolved concerning slavery and the power to be given to states of different sizes. However, the delegates generally favored a stronger federal government, and this helped to keep the discussions moving forward.

The Constitution begins with a statement of purpose called the *Preamble.* In the Preamble, the writers explain why the United States needs to be governed by the simple rules set forth in the Constitution.

✍ Read the Preamble (page 70).

In the blanks below, rewrite each phrase of the Preamble in your own words. Consult a dictionary if you need help with the vocabulary.

We the people of the United States: _____

in order to form a more perfect union: _____

establish justice: _____

insure domestic tranquility: _____

provide for the common defense: _____

promote the general welfare: _____

and secure the blessings of liberty to ourselves and our posterity:

_____

do ordain and establish this Constitution for the United States of America:

_____

Take Another Look

Who, What, Where, When, Why

Investigate the circumstances surrounding the writing of the Constitution at the Constitutional Convention. Where and when did the Constitutional Convention take place? Who wrote the Constitution? Why did these men want to write a new Constitution? What did they come up with—a revised Articles of Confederation or a whole new document?

Make a five W's wheel displaying the historical information you found in researching the answers to the *who*, *what*, *where*, *when*, and *why* questions.

Many Leaders, Many Talents

We all know about Benjamin Franklin and George Washington. We probably know a little about Alexander Hamilton and James Madison, too. But there were other colonial leaders at the Constitutional Convention about whom we have a lot to learn.

Identify another leader who was there and research him. Now pretend that it is 1787 and you are a reporter on the local paper. You have been hired to write a story about that leader. The Constitution has just been written, and the country is looking to newspapers to inform it about the writers of the Constitution. What will you write? What was this leader's role at the convention? Was he from a large state or a small state? How did that affect his views? What did he want included in the Constitution? What did he want excluded? How did his presence at the convention make a difference to the document as finally written?

Being a Citizen

Now that you have identified what the Preamble means, think about how its words relate to you as an individual. Think of yourself as a citizen at the time of the writing of the Constitution. In 1787, you were glad to be finished with the war against England and tired of bickering colonies, each concerned with losing power to a common union. You were also hopeful of a good life without unfair English taxes and laws.

Which of the stated purposes in the Preamble might have been most important to you then? Now, as a citizen today, which of the stated purposes seems most important?

Write a short essay explaining your thoughts about which Preamble purpose might have seemed the most important then and now.

ARTICLE I
The Legislative Branch
ℰ
What Is the Legislative Branch and Who Can Serve?

The legislative branch is made up of the Congress, which has the power to make new laws and to change old ones. This power to make laws is given to the two groups of lawmakers that make up the Congress, the Senate and the House of Representatives.

The Senate

The Senate is made up of two senators from each state, regardless of the number of people living in that state. Senators serve for a period of years called a *term*.

ℰ Read Article I, Section III, Clause 1 (page 71). The senators' terms are staggered so that every two years only one-third of the senators are up for election.

How long is the term of a senator? Why is staggering terms a good idea?

_____

ℰ Read the 17th Amendment (pages 82–83). Under the 17th Amendment, which is still in effect today, who selects senators to represent states in the Senate?

_____

The House of Representatives

The number of representatives each state has in the House of Representatives is based on the state's population. States that have more people living in them elect more representatives to serve in the House. Representatives serve for ____ years.

ℰ Read Article I, Section II, Clause 3 (page 70). When the Constitution was written, the writers argued about how to count slaves for tax and representation purposes. They agreed on the "three-fifths compromise." How did they count the slaves?

_____

ℰ Read the 13th Amendment (page 81). How did this amendment affect the three-fifths compromise?

_____

Take Another Look

Who Can Run for Office?

The following sections of the Constitution describe the minimum qualifications for the positions of representative and senator:

ᔐ Read Article I, Section II, Clause 2 (page 70).

ᔐ Read Article I, Section III, Clause 3 (page 71).

Make a chart comparing the qualifications of senators and representatives.

Whom Should We Nominate?

Divide into small groups. Pretend you are members of a nominating committee. Choose either a real or fictitious representative or senator. Create and perform skits of your nomination discussions. In your skits, state how your chosen candidate meets the minimum requirements. Refer to issues the candidate has public opinions on that you think are important. Talk about your candidate's prior experience (for example, whether he or she held an elected or appointed office, is a lawyer or a business person within the community, and so forth). For information about your elected representatives, refer to the *Congressional Directory* (which includes field office and biographical information), published by the U.S. Government Printing Office, or contact your local library to find Web site information.

Being a Citizen

Choose an issue which you think is important. Look around your community. Is there a problem you see that needs addressing? Do you see homeless people? Is there violence that concerns you? Are the schools as good as they should be? Write a letter to your representative asking what position he or she holds on the problem and how his or her work in Congress can help solve the problem. If you know where your representative stands on an issue, offer solutions to help him or her succeed.

When Congress Is in Session, Who Takes the Lead?

The House of Representatives and the Senate are each made up of many members. They are required to meet once each year. The 20th Amendment provides that the meeting begins in January and continues during weekdays for much of the rest of the year, with occasional days off for vacation and holidays. When you read in the newspaper that Congress is "in session," it means that this yearly meeting is underway.

The writers of the Constitution knew that someone needed to lead these meetings. They provided for this in the Constitution.

The following sections of the Constitution give the title of the person who presides over, or leads, the annual sessions of each house of Congress.

✍ Read Article I, Section II, Clause 5 (page 71). Who presides over the House of Representatives?

_____

✍ Read Article I, Section III, Clause 4 (page 71). Who presides over the Senate?

_____

✍ Read Article I, Section III, Clause 5 (page 71). Who takes over in this person's absence?

_____

In addition to those who preside over the congressional sessions, there are other leaders in each house of Congress as well. There are two leaders in each house for each of the two major political parties—Republican and Democrat. In each house, one party is the *majority* party and one party is the *minority* party. If there are more Democrats than Republicans in that house, the Democratic Party is the majority party. If there are more Republicans, the Republican Party is the majority party. Each time there is an election, the *majority position* in each house has the possibility of changing.

For each party in each house, there is a majority leader or a minority leader. In each house, the members of each party choose these leaders from among themselves. The person chosen is usually a member with some experience in Congress. There is also another "assistant" leader for each party called a *whip*.

These positions are not required by the Constitution. They have developed over the years to help each party's members discuss positions on issues and exchange information.

We the People, Copyright © Pamela A. Marx

Take Another Look

Who's in Charge Here?

Create an organizational chart of the positions of leadership in each house of Congress. Find out who currently holds these positions and identify the leaders by name. Identify the current majority and minority party for each house of Congress. List the majority and minority leader and whips for each party.

Good resources for this project are the field office of your local representative, the *Congressional Directory* published by the U.S. Government Printing Office, and an almanac.

We're in Session

Television channels such as C-SPAN air congressional sessions and hearings. Movies such as "Mr. Smith Goes to Washington" dramatize fictional congressional proceedings. The *Congressional Record* provides a record of congressional proceedings.

- Visit the *Congressional Record* on the Internet through http://www.access.gpo.gov/su_docs/aces/aces150.html. Work with a group to write a script of a representative requesting permission of the speaker to introduce a proposed law in the House. Perform your script with classmates.

Being a Citizen

There are many demands on a representative or senator's time. In addition to attending Congressional sessions, he or she may attend a hearing on a proposed law, visit home to attend a community forum, or research issues of importance. What do you think are good reasons to miss part of a session of Congress? Do you think it is important to attend when it is time to vote on a proposed law?

Imagine you are Representative Doe. Next Wednesday there is a vote scheduled in the House on a tax law that will increase income taxes if passed. This is a law about which voters in your district are very concerned. Some months ago you committed yourself to attend an assembly at a school in your district that same day to present a new United States flag. Think about how you should handle this conflict. What would your voters want you to do? If you decide to cancel your trip home, write a letter to the school explaining why. If you decide to skip the vote, write an open letter to voters in your district explaining why.

Membership in Congress—Conduct, Privileges, and Restrictions

As of the year 2000, there are 435 representatives in the House of Representatives. The number of people who live in a state determines how many representatives that state can elect. States that have more people send more representatives to the House of Representatives.

ℝ Read Article I, Section II, Clause 3 (page 70). How often is the "actual enumeration" of people in each state done?

_____

When was the last census done? _____

Senators and representatives have certain privileges. They receive a yearly salary and can vote on the amount of that salary. The 27th Amendment says that any salary change Congress votes on cannot become effective until the next election of representatives has taken place. Why is this a good idea?

Another privilege that each senator or representative has is that, unless he or she commits treason, a felony (serious crime), or a breach of the peace, that member is free from arrest when Congress is in session. The writers of the Constitution included this provision so that it would be difficult for people who disagreed with representatives' views to keep them from attending Congress and from voting on important bills without good reason.

Article I gives each house of Congress authority to "seat" members of its own house—that is, to review the election process, returns, and qualifications of its members. In addition, once it has accepted members as qualified, each house of Congress must run its meetings and other business by the rules it adopts. Each house also decides when and how to punish one of its own members for "disorderly behavior"—that is, for breaking the rules.

ℝ Read Article I, Section V, Clause 2 (page 72). What vote is required to expel a member?

_____

Both the House and the Senate are required to keep a "journal" of their proceedings and to publish it so that the public can learn about what Congress is doing. This journal—called the *Congressional Record*—is published daily.

ℝ Read Article I, Section V, Clause 3 (page 72). What information must the *Congressional Record* include?

_____

Take Another Look

Who Represents Me?

Now that you know a little bit about your federal government and the structure of the Congress, see what you can find out about your state government. Is the state legislature made up of one house (*unicameral*) or two houses (*bicameral*)?

Find out the name or names of that house (or houses) and who your representatives are. Create a flow chart to present this information about your state on a poster. Include the name of your state's chief executive, the governor. One resource for some of this information is *The World Almanac and Book of Facts*.

On the Floor

Break into small groups and review a portion of the *Congressional Record*. The *Congressional Record* can be located through the Government Printing Office at U.S. Government Printing Office, Superintendent of Documents, Mail Stop SSOP, Washington, D.C. 20402-9328; 202-512-1800 or 888-293-6498; http://www.access.gpo.gov/su_docs/aces/aces150.html.

Choose an interesting discussion, vote, or speech. Research the background of the subject and reenact a scene based on it.

Being a Citizen

When the representative of your congressional district votes on a bill, he or she is representing you and your community. How can you find out what your representative thinks about different issues on which he or she votes?

Call the local field office of your congressional representative, and ask if he or she sends voters any periodic publications about what is happening in Washington, D.C. If so, ask the office to send you a copy of the most recent one. Also ask the staff member what methods the representative uses to find out how the voters in his or her district feel about the issues. Review the publication you receive. Write a two-paragraph essay on one subject on which your congressional representative has expressed his or her views, indicating whether you agree or disagree. Also discuss whether you feel the representative's methods for collecting information are sufficient.

How Congress Makes Law

Any law passed by Congress begins as a bill in the House of Representatives or the Senate. A bill is a proposed law. Anyone can have an idea for a bill, but once it is written, a member of either the House or Senate must present it to that house during a session. The bill then proceeds as follows.

Once a bill is introduced into either the House or Senate chamber, it is sent to a committee that studies what the bill says, how it will work as law, and what effects, intended and unintended, it might have. As part of this "study" process, the committee can hold hearings and ask experts and interested people to give their opinions ("testimony") about what is good and what is bad about the proposed law. The bill may be changed as a result of these hearings. The committee then votes on the modified bill.

If the committee approves the bill, it goes back to the chamber from which it came for a vote by all members. If the bill is approved by a majority of that chamber, it goes to the other congressional chamber for review by another committee, which may make changes, and then vote on it. If approved by that committee, the bill is voted on by the members of that chamber.

Since the bill may have been changed in the second committee, the bill returns to the chamber in which it was first introduced. This chamber reviews the changes made to the bill, then votes on it again. If all the changes are approved, it goes to the president for signature. If some compromise is needed, a joint committee with members from each chamber might be formed to rewrite certain parts of the bill. Once this is done, each chamber votes on it again. If a majority in each chamber approves it once again, the bill goes to the president.

∽ Read Article I, Section VII, Clause 1 (page 72). What one kind of bill must start in the House of Representatives, not the Senate?

_____

∽ Read Article I, Section V, Clause 1 (page 72). A *quorum* (minimum number) of representatives must be present in order for a house of Congress to conduct business. How many lawmakers must be present?

_____

∽ Read Article I, Section VII, Clause 2 (page 72). Once a bill passes both houses of Congress and the president signs it, the bill becomes law. If the president does not want the bill to become law, he or she can *veto* it, or refuse to approve it. How can the president do this?

_____

For Congress to pass a bill after a veto, both chambers must vote for it by a two-thirds majority.

We the People, Copyright © Pamela A. Marx

Take Another Look

Write Your Own Bill

Turn your class into Congress. Form groups of six students each. Identify half of the groups as members of the Senate and half of the groups as members of the House. Have each group write a proposed law about something the group wants to change about school life, the community, or an issue of national importance. Each group should discuss the bill, making it as clear as possible.

Bills introduced into the Senate are called "S. [insert number]" and bills introduced into the House are called "H.R. [insert number]." Give each bill a number like the bills in Congress.

Congress Is in Session

This activity is a follow-up to the preceding activity. Once each group has written its bill, turn your class into the two houses of Congress. Those who were members of the House of Representatives should gather as that chamber in one part of the room, and those who were members of the Senate should gather as that chamber in another part of the room.

Have each half conduct a mock session of its chamber for the class. In this session, the bill of an individual group will be introduced by number and described. Each chamber can vote on its bill and send it to the other chamber. After the chambers swap bills, they read the other's bill, make any changes they choose, vote on these changes, and send them back. Have each chamber keep track of the members' votes as required by Article I, Section VII, Clause 2. The bills then go to a person chosen to act as the president for signature or veto.

Being a Citizen

Read the national news section of the newspaper or a news magazine such as *Time, Newsweek,* or *U.S. News and World Report* to find an article describing a bill pending in Congress. Write a brief description of the bill, and then state your opinion about whether the bill should become law based on how it will affect you and your community.

Impeachment

Impeachment is the act of accusing a public official of misconduct in office by bringing charges before an appropriate body. Article I gives Congress the right to impeach the president and other high officials of the executive and judicial branches. The process begins when the House of Representatives investigates charges of misconduct. If it decides there was misconduct, it sends an accusation to the Senate that an official has done something which it believes violates the oath of office.

✍ Read Article II, Section IV (page 76). On what grounds can the president or vice-president be impeached?

_____

Once the Senate receives the accusation from the House, it must hold a trial. If the official is found guilty by a two-thirds vote of the Senate, he or she is removed from office and is disqualified from holding any other office of trust in the United States.

Impeachment is a very serious issue. In 1868, Andrew Johnson was impeached for firing one of his cabinet members, which was in violation of a law that Congress had passed. Since then there has been significant discussion about possible impeachment of only two presidents. One of these was Richard M. Nixon, who resigned from office before he was impeached, due to what became known as the "Watergate scandal." The other president, William Clinton, was impeached for perjury (lying under oath) and obstruction of justice. Judges have also been impeached for various kinds of misconduct.

✍ Read Article I, Section III, Clause 6 (page 71). If the president is on trial as a result of an impeachment, who presides over the trial in the Senate?

_____

This official is from the Supreme Court.

How many of the senators must vote for conviction in order to find the impeached (or accused) official guilty?

_____

✍ Read Article I, Section III, Clause 7 (page 71). What is the punishment for conviction at the Senate trial on impeachment?

_____

What can happen to an official after he or she is convicted?

_____

Take Another Look

Questions of Impeachment

Richard Nixon resigned as president in August, 1974, after what became known as the Watergate scandal. Find out what questions of wrongdoing were raised in connection with him. Based on your research, decide if you think the House of Representatives would have been justified in impeaching Nixon. Write a two-paragraph essay explaining your position.

Deciding Andrew Johnson's Fate

Form groups of four students. It is 1868. Your group must decide whether or not to vote to impeach Andrew Johnson. Base your decision on the following facts.

- Edwin Stanton, Johnson's Secretary of War, is a member of Johnson's cabinet, but he has also been spying on Johnson and supplying information to the members of the Radical Party in Congress. Because of this, Johnson does not think Stanton is a good cabinet member. Johnson is about to fire him.

- Before Johnson can fire Stanton, the Radicals in Congress pass a law called the Tenure of Office Act, which makes it illegal for Johnson to fire Stanton without the Senate's consent.

- Johnson thinks this law is unconstitutional. Based upon this belief, Johnson fires Stanton, despite the law. Johnson is now before the House of Representatives for an impeachment vote.

Discuss the pros and cons of impeaching Johnson. Take a vote within your group on whether or not to impeach. Compare your group's decision with those of the other groups in your class.

Being a Citizen

Public opinion was divided on the House of Representatives' impeachment hearings of William Clinton in 1998. Many people felt that what he did wrong was not serious enough to interfere with his job as president.

The crimes listed in Article II, Section IV are vague. Decide what "high crime or misdemeanor" is serious enough for an official to be removed from office. Is drunk driving? Is burglary?

The Express Powers of the Legislative Branch

Article I, Section VIII of the Constitution contains 17 clauses that describe the powers of Congress. These powers are called the *express powers* because each clause describes specific responsibilities. For example, Clause 5 gives Congress the power to coin money and establish the value of each coin.

✍ Read Article I, Section VIII, Clauses 1 through 17 (pages 73–74). Write which clause gives Congress each of the powers described below.

Just as a person borrows money to buy a house, the United States government must borrow money from time to time to pay for the work of the government. This clause gives Congress the authorization to borrow this money.

_____

We have a large country with many individual states. People in different states do business with each other. States enter into contracts and do business with each other. This is called *commerce.* The United States enters into contracts called *treaties* with other countries for business and trade. This clause gives Congress the power to make rules about commerce and to approve treaties that the president negotiates.

_____

Interstate highways are major roads that cross through many states. Post offices deliver mail in each state in the country. This clause gives Congress the power to establish highways and post offices.

_____

People who write music and books own the rights to their work. These rights are called *copyrights.* People who discover new inventions own the rights to their inventions. These rights are called *patents.* Congress is responsible for promoting the arts and sciences by making laws through this clause that give copyright and patent holders the right to use what they create without interference from others for a specific number of years.

_____

Take Another Look

Congressional Power in Action

Choose one of the powers of Congress described in Section VIII and find out more about it. An example of an idea for investigation is researching patents and copyrights. What are the names of the government offices where these rights are filed and reviewed? How long do copyrights and patents last? Can they be extended? Is computer software copyrighted or patented?

What Is Interstate Commerce?

Under the commerce clause, Congress has the power to make rules about interstate commerce. Commerce is the buying and selling of products and the transporting of those products from place to place. *Interstate* means between and among the states. This might sound like Congress can only make laws about products sent from one state to another, such as a car made in Detroit, Michigan, then sold in Savannah, Georgia. However, Congress has used the commerce clause to regulate actions *within* states if it can show that those individual actions, when taken together with other individual actions, have a broad affect across state lines. Consider this situation:

In the 1960s, Congress passed the Civil Rights Act. Part of this Act prohibited racial discrimination in restaurants that sold food which might be eaten on the premises by interstate travelers. This Act also prohibited racial discrimination if a substantial part of the food served had moved in interstate commerce. Congress based its right to regulate discrimination in local restaurants on its commerce clause power. The owner of a restaurant called Ollie's Barbeque challenged the law.

Write a paragraph on how you feel about Congress making a law that tells a restaurant owner who he or she must serve in his or her restaurant. Is such a law justified if Congress is protecting people from discrimination? (See *Katzenburg* v. *McClung*, pages 66–67).

Being a Citizen

We are connected to people all across the country. We rely on them, and they rely on us. Consider food. A person buying flour in California helps a farmer earn a living in Kansas. This is one reason why it is important for our elected representatives to talk with other representatives. Make a chart of five different aspects of your daily life which rely on people across state lines.

The "Elastic Clause" and the Implied Powers of Congress

Article I, Section VIII, Clause 18, gives Congress the power to make "all laws which shall be necessary and proper" for carrying out the express powers of Congress. This clause is sometimes called the "necessary and proper" clause. It is also referred to as the "elastic clause." The men who wrote the Constitution knew that it would have to be *flexible* enough to meet the needs of a growing country.

List three ways in which the country has changed since the adoption of the Constitution.

_____

_____

_____

Does this clause let Congress adopt any law it wants? No, of course not. Laws it passes must be necessary to carry out its express powers under the Constitution. The Constitution is structured so that if Congress passes a law that is not allowable under the Constitution, the president may veto it. The Supreme Court may also review laws to determine if they fall within the guidelines of the Constitution.

The Supreme Court has also interpreted the express powers of Congress to include certain *implied* powers that are necessary to carry out those *express* powers. How could the idea of implied powers cause trouble between representatives of the states and representatives of the federal government?

_____

_____

In 1816, Congress used its implied powers to create a national bank. When the bank's representative in Maryland refused to pay a state tax, Maryland sued the bank representative. It argued that Congress did not have the power to create the bank in the first place. (See *McCulloch* v. *Maryland*, page 67). The Supreme Court found that the creation of the bank was constitutional. Its creation was needed to help carry out Congress's express powers to collect taxes and borrow money. This famous case made clear that Congress has implied powers to do things that are not specifically prohibited by the Constitution if those things further its express powers.

Take Another Look

An Implied Power Law

Justice Marshall wrote this about deciding whether an act of Congress was within its implied powers: "[If] the end be legitimate, [if] it be within the scope of the constitution, [then] all means appropriate...are constitutional."

Would it have made sense for the writers of the Constitution to try to list every single thing that Congress had the power to do?

Pretend you are Justice Marshall. Write a letter to a law student. Explain the above quote and how it helps Congress do its job.

Expanding Federal Power and the Moonshiners

Conflicts grew between those who believed in a loose (or *broad*) interpretation of the powers the federal government had under the Constitution, and those who believed in a strict (or *narrow*) interpretation, which limited the power of the federal government. In Pennsylvania, the Whiskey Rebellion of 1794 challenged the power of the federal government to impose a tax on homemade whiskey. Pennsylvanians drove tax collectors out of town and tarred and feathered them. They believed the federal government had no right to impose the tax. Washington was forced to call out federal troops.

Research the Whiskey Rebellion and create an eight-panel storyboard of the story of this rebellion. (A storyboard is a series of illustrations with text.)

Being a Citizen

Even though there is no express power to protect the flag, Congress passed the Federal Flag Protection Act of 1989. This law said that anyone who "knowingly mutilates, defaces, physically defiles, burns, maintains on the floor or ground, or tramples upon any flag of the United States" can be fined or imprisoned.

What do you think the authors of the Constitution would have thought of this law? Pretend you are a descendant of one of the writers of the Constitution. Write an editorial for the local paper about what you think your ancestor would think about this law. Would he agree with it, or would he think this law went against the personal freedoms the Constitution tried to insure for each citizen? (See *United States* v. *Eichman*, page 68.)

Prohibitions on the Powers of Congress and the States

The framers of the Constitution decided that there were certain things they wanted to be very sure Congress did not try to do.

∽ Read Article I, Section IX, Clause 1 (page 74). Slavery was a big sticking point in writing the Constitution. The representatives from those states in which plantation owners relied on slaves to work the fields did not want the new Constitution to let Congress outlaw slave trading. Those who wanted to make slave trading illegal compromised. Until what year did this clause prohibit Congress from abolishing the slave trade?

_____

∽ Read Article I, Section IX, Clause 2 (page 74). According to this clause, which privilege can no branch of the federal government suspend except in cases of rebellion or public danger?

_____

This privilege allows a person being detained to receive an immediate court review of whether or not he or she is being legally held.

∽ Read Article I, Section IX, Clause 3 (page 74). When King George had control over the colonies, he passed *bills of attainder* and *ex post facto laws*. A *bill of attainder* is a law that is made to punish a certain person. It is not a law that applies to all people. Congress cannot make a law that says one person cannot do something that other people can do. An *ex post facto* law is one that makes it illegal for a person to have done something that was not illegal when he or she did it. For example, suppose you ride your bike on Monday, May 1st. On Tuesday, May 2nd, a law is passed that makes it illegal to ride a bike, but the law is said to be effective as of Monday, May 1st. According to this law, the police could legally come and give you a ticket. Article I, Section X prohibits states from passing these two kinds of laws as well as laws impairing obligations under contracts.

∽ Read the 16th Amendment (page 82). Article I, Section IX, Clauses 4 and 5 tell Congress how it can and cannot pass tax laws. The Sixteenth Amendment modified Clause 4. On what does this amendment allow Congress to collect taxes?

_____

Take Another Look

In a State of Crisis

When Abraham Lincoln was president, the Civil War broke out. At the time, Congress was not in session. Lincoln felt that, in order to preserve the union, he had to take immediate action—even if his actions were inconsistent with the Constitution. These are some of the steps he took:

- He suspended the writ of habeas corpus so that those who were against the union could be detained without a hearing.
- Without the authorization of Congress, he increased the size of the federal army.
- Without the authorization of Congress, he directed the Treasury Department to advance $2 million to private citizens for military purposes.

Work in small groups to decide which clauses of Article I, Sections VIII and IX, Lincoln's actions violated, who (if anyone) had the power to do what Lincoln did, and whether the president was justified in his actions.

Being a Citizen

Dissatisfaction with taxes is one of the most common complaints of citizens in the United States. People complain that they are forced to pay too much and that the money is spent unwisely.

Evidence of the many ways in which federal tax money is used is all around you. For example, money from federal taxes is used in our schools, to repair our highways, to pay soldiers' wages in the military, and to buy military equipment.

Talk with three adults you know. Poll each of them to find out three things on which he or she is happiest to have his or her tax dollars spent. What three things do you think are the most important things on which to spend tax money? Write an essay comparing the results of your poll with your own opinions on how tax money should be spent.

ARTICLE II
Executive Department

Election and Term of Office

Article II describes the powers of the executive branch of the government. The president of the United States is the Chief Executive of this branch. The president and the departments of government that report to him or her are responsible for carrying out the laws that Congress passes.

∽ Read Article II, Section I, Clause 1 (page 75). Each time the president is elected, he or she serves for a term of office. How long is a term?

_____

When the Constitution was written, it included no limit on the number of terms a president could serve. George Washington did not run after his second term. All the presidents after him followed his example until Franklin D. Roosevelt, who was elected to four terms. The 22nd Amendment limited the number of times a person could be elected president.

∽ Read the 22nd Amendment (page 84). How many times may a person be elected to serve as president?

_____

When the Constitution was adopted, many people in the United States could not read or write, so the framers decided that a special process was needed to make sure that educated people determined who would be president.

∽ Read Article II, Section I, Clause 2 (page 75). What does each state appoint to vote for the president?

_____

Each state's legislature decides how these people are selected. Together, these people are called the Electoral College. They still elect the president today. Today, the people of each state choose their representatives to the Electoral College by voting on a ballot for a presidential candidate.

An early amendment to the Constitution changed the method for electing the president. Which amendment did this?

_____

We the People, Copyright © Pamela A. Marx

Take Another Look

It's Time for a Change

Franklin Roosevelt was elected to serve four terms of office as president (1933-1945). Roosevelt was president during the Great Depression and World War II. Since Roosevelt was elected to serve for four terms, we can assume that the majority of the American voters wanted him to stay in office. Yet, despite his successes and popularity, many people thought his long period of service was a problem and pushed to change the Constitution.

Pretend that the debate concerning the adoption of the 22nd Amendment has just gotten under way. Divide the class in half. One half works on reasons why we might want a president in office for more than eight years. The other half works on reasons for having a frequent change of president. Then debate the issue as a class.

Problem in the Electoral College

The Electoral College still votes to determine who will be president. The Electoral College vote is almost always consistent with the popular vote by ballot of the American people. Generally, if a candidate wins the ballot vote, he or she also wins the Electoral College vote, but in the presidential election of 1888, the candidate who won the popular vote lost the Electoral College vote.

Investigate the 1888 election. Work in small groups to write and present a newscast of your findings. In your newscast, give your opinion on whether the Electoral College should be abolished.

Being a Citizen

Voting for president is an important responsibility. For many decades, the president has been the most powerful person in the world.

Sometimes people say that a candidate is a good, honest person, but has no charisma so people will not listen to him or her. Is being honest more or less important than being charismatic? Brainstorm as a class the three most important qualities of a good presidential candidate.

Presidential Qualifications and Vacancies

↪ Read Article II, Section I, Clause 4 (page 75). What are the three qualifications required for a person to run for president of the United States?

_____

_____

↪ Read Article II, Section I, Clause 5 (page 75). This clause states what the framers thought should happen if a president becomes unable to serve out a term. Who takes over for the president?

_____

The framers also provided a framework for what would happen if both the president and vice-president became unable to serve. Who decides what officer will act as president should both become unable to serve?

_____

The 25th Amendment was passed to give more guidance about what happens when a vice-president becomes president. This amendment was passed because the public became concerned after the 1963 assassination of President John F. Kennedy. Vice-President Lyndon Baines Johnson was sworn in as president, leaving the vice-presidency vacant.

↪ Read Amendment 25, Section 2 (page 85). When there is a vacancy in the vice-president's position, who nominates someone to fill the position?

_____

Before the person nominated to be vice-president can take office, both houses of Congress must vote on the appointment. What kind of vote is required by both houses to approve the appointment?

_____

Sections 3 and 4 of the 25th Amendment (page 85) describe what happens if the president becomes temporarily unable to serve. If the president is able, who must he or she notify that he or she is unable to serve and who takes over for the president?

_____

_____

Take Another Look

Comparing Qualifications

The qualifications for running for president are different from those described in the Constitution for persons who want to run for the House of Representatives or the Senate. One of the requirements for the office of president is that the person be a natural-born citizen. Find out how this is different from being a *naturalized* citizen. Is there a requirement that senators and representatives be natural-born citizens? Make a chart comparing the qualifications for the presidency, Senate, and House of Representatives.

Before We Knew It

The 25th Amendment was passed to clarify what would happen when the vice-president's position was vacated. To everyone's surprise, it was vacated again in 1973 when Vice-President Spiro Agnew resigned. Congress looked to its own to fill the vacancy left by Agnew's resignation. The person who filled Agnew's position ultimately became president of the United States. Research who this was and how it happened. Write a one-paragraph report describing this historical twist of fate and give your opinion as to whether or not Congress made a good decision in looking where it did to replace the vice-president.

Being a Citizen

The Constitution says nothing about the education a person must have to run for president of the United States. People from many different walks of life have served as president. Many of them have been lawyers.

Find out more about the people who have held the position of president. Work with a partner to do a random survey of 10 presidents of the nineteenth and twentieth centuries.

How many served previously in Congress? Did they hold other elected offices? How many were farmers, lawyers, or business people? Decide upon at least five questions to investigate about the presidents you research; turn your results into a graph showing each president's prior experience. Do the results of your research surprise you, or are they what you expected?

The Powers of the President

As the head of the executive branch of the government, the president fulfills many roles.

✍ Read Article II, Section II, Clause 1 (page 76). The president is the person to whom the American armed forces report. These forces include the Army, Navy, Air Force, and Marines. When acting as the leader of the armed services, what is the president called?

_____

The president needs advice on a continuing basis to do a good job. The president has a cabinet made up of men and women who are experts in different fields. They run large departments that implement the laws that Congress passes. In these departments, thousands of employees work under the cabinet members. The employees gather information and handle problems as they arise. The cabinet member in charge of each department is called the *secretary of the department*, and he or she gives the president advice on important issues.

The president also has the power to grant reprieves and pardons of individuals convicted of crimes against the United States. When does the president *not* have the authority to grant a pardon?

_____

✍ Read Article II, Section II, Clause 2 (page 76). This section gives the president other important powers. In some cases, the president can exercise these powers, but he or she must get the consent of the Senate in the choices he or she makes. For example, the president has the power to negotiate treaties. *Treaties* are agreements with foreign countries. They can be about trade between the countries, boundary disputes, and other important issues. Who must approve the president's treaties before they become effective and by what margin of vote?

_____

The president nominates and, with Senate approval, appoints certain kinds of officers of the United States government. Some serve in foreign countries. Some serve in the courts. List three of the kinds of officers the president can nominate.

_____

_____

_____

Take Another Look

Who's in Charge?

Throughout the history of the United States, presidents have appointed ministers and ambassadors to foreign countries. Find out more about one of the following past ambassadors. Write a speech to introduce that individual. Let the audience know why the president nominated this person to serve.

Charles Francis Adams
Shirley Temple Black

Jeane Kirkpatrick
Robert Livingston

Averell Harriman
Andrew Young

Congress Versus the President

Who do you think has the greater power over the military—the president or Congress? As you think about this, remember that Congress—not the president—has the power to declare war. However, American troops have fought repeatedly on foreign soil in "nonwars" such as the Korean War, the Vietnam War, and the Gulf War. In each of these "police actions," as they are sometimes called, the president authorized troops to be sent without a congressional declaration of war.

Choose one "nonwar" to research. Find out more about how and why troops were sent to fight. What do you think of the decision to fight the war you researched? Write a one-page report about the "police action" you researched. Describe how the use of American troops came about, and give your opinion about its appropriateness.

Being a Citizen

There are many different executive departments, each headed by a cabinet member who is called the *secretary*. Some of these departments are the Department of Justice, the Department of the Treasury, the Department of Defense, and the Department of Education

Pretend you are looking for a job. Decide which department you would like to work for, why it would be interesting to work there, and what you would like to achieve. Write a sample letter to the head of this department explaining why you want to work there.

ARTICLE III
The Judicial Branch

The "What" and "Who" of the Judicial Branch

The judicial system created by Article III is a system of federal courts. In addition to this system of courts, each state has a set of courts. Section I of Article III of the Constitution names only one court, the highest court in the land, but it provides for the creation of other lower courts.

Read Article III, Section I (page 77). What is the name given to the highest court in the land?

_____

What body can establish inferior, or lower, courts, such as trial courts?

_____

The Constitution states that judges in the federal courts "shall hold their offices during good behavior." This means that judges are appointed for life as long as they do not act in ways inconsistent with their office. If they do engage in wrongful behavior, they can be removed from their judicial positions by the impeachment process.

Judges have been impeached and removed from office for certain kinds of lying and other behavior that is not consistent with the laws they are charged with upholding. Research the subject of impeachment and find three other charges for which judges have been impeached. List the charges here.

_____

_____

_____

Judges are paid for serving the court system. What does Article III, Section I, say about a judge's pay while he or she serves in office?

_____

Can you think of one reason why the writers of the Constitution included this rule about a judge's pay?

_____

Take Another Look

A Job for Life

Think about the job that judges do. It is important that they be fair in their decisions. We do not want our judges to be afraid to make decisions because those decisions might be unpopular with some members of the community. We want them to make decisions consistent with the Constitution and the law.

Work with a partner to create a chart of the advantages and disadvantages of appointing a judge for life versus electing a judge periodically. Consider these questions: Which system is more likely to make a judge worry about whether his or her decisions are popular? What happens when a judge gets lazy about doing his or her job? What happens when a judge becomes ill?

What Do You Think?

Once you have created the chart suggested by the above activity, work in groups of three or four to role-play some of the issues that lifetime versus elected terms raise. Will you role-play a situation in which a judge makes an inappropriate decision because of an upcoming election? Perhaps the judge is presiding over a controversial criminal case in which the public has a strong interest in a severe punishment for the defendant. How could this affect the judge's decision? Another situation might be a Supreme Court justice who has a tendency to fall asleep when listening to the oral arguments made by attorneys.

Being a Citizen

What do you think should be considered a "high crime and misdemeanor" for which a judge could be removed from office? Should he or she be impeached for breaking *any* law? There are many kinds of laws. Consider these possibilities: robbery, shoplifting, driving over the speed limit, drunk driving, taking illegal drugs, hitting or abusing a spouse, or taking a bribe.

Pick a selection of illegal acts and survey 10 people. Ask each of them which of your selection of illegal acts he or she feels should be reasons to impeach a judge. Graph your survey results.

All Kinds of Cases

There are two basic types of federal court cases: criminal and civil. In *criminal* courts, a person who is accused of breaking a law (the *defendant*) is brought before the court. It is the job of the attorney for the government to prove that the defendant committed the crime. *Civil* courts hear other kinds of cases arising under federal laws.

✎ Read Article III, Section II, Clause 1 (page 77). List three kinds of cases over which the federal courts have jurisdiction.

_____

_____

The 11th Amendment changed part of this clause to bar a citizen of one state from suing another state in federal court unless that state consents, but it does not bar Supreme Court review of cases or cases brought against subdivisions of a state or state officials accused of violating a person's constitutional rights.

✎ Read Article III, Section II, Clause 2 (page 77). This clause describes the two basic kinds of Supreme Court jurisdiction. What kind of jurisdiction does the Supreme Court have in cases involving ambassadors from foreign countries?

_____

What other kinds of jurisdiction does this court have?

_____

✎ Read Article III, Section II, Clause 3 (page 77). What kinds of cases must be tried by a jury? Where must these trials be held? Why?

_____

_____

✎ Read Article III, Section III, Clause 1 (page 77). Treason is the act of bringing war against one's own country or helping its enemies. An *overt act* is a clear and specific act. To find a person guilty of the crime of treason, how many witnesses must testify to the "same overt act"?

_____

Take Another Look

Original and Appellate Courts

When a court has *original* jurisdiction over a case, that court hears the case the first time it is presented and makes a decision. When a court has *appellate* jurisdiction over a case, the case is first heard in another court, and the appellate court reviews what the first court did. The trial court in the federal system is called the *district court*. For cases that begin in the district court, the process generally works like this:

Federal district courts—These are trial courts which have only original jurisdiction. These courts do not review the decisions of other courts. They hear cases for the first time and review both the facts (or evidence) presented and how the law applies to those facts. A decision is then made.

Circuit courts of appeals—These courts have appellate jurisdiction. If a party is unhappy with a decision made in district court, the party can appeal the case—that is, ask for review by the court of appeals. These courts do not look at new evidence. They review what happened in the trial court and decide if there were any mistakes in how that court applied the law.

Supreme Court—This court has original jurisdiction of some cases, but spends most of its time on cases over which it has appellate jurisdiction. If a party is unhappy with the decision of the court of appeals, the party can ask the Supreme Court to review the case. Because there are so many cases and so many appeals filed, the Supreme Court can review only a handful of the appeals it receives. If it refuses to hear the appeal, the decision of the court of appeals stands. If it agrees to hear the case, it will make a decision. It reviews only those cases that it believes involve issues of law that need to be interpreted or clarified.

Find three articles from a local newspaper on different court cases. Determine whether each case is in the federal court system or the state court system. For each case, decide whether it involves original or appellate jurisdiction.

Being a Citizen

In the 1950s, Julius and Ethel Rosenberg were convicted of treason and sentenced to death in a controversial case that arose during the time of the "red scare." They were the only people ever executed in peacetime in the United States for the crime of espionage.

Research this case and write an editorial based on the results of your investigation. Include your opinion on the justness of the outcome.

We the People, Copyright © Pamela A. Marx

The Power of Judicial Review

In the 1800s, President John Adams, a member of the Federalist Party, lost his reelection bid to Thomas Jefferson. In an attempt to give the Federalists power even after he left office, Adams signed the appointments of many "midnight judges" who shared his Federalist views, including one for William Marbury. Though signed, many of the appointments were not delivered when the new secretary of state under Jefferson, James Madison, took office. When Marbury realized Madison was never going to deliver the papers to make his judgeship official, he went to the Supreme Court and asked for a writ to get the papers delivered. He asked for the writ under the Judiciary Act of 1789 that Congress had passed, which gave the Supreme Court the right to issue such writs. Chief Justice John Marshall looked at the act under which Marbury sued for the writ and the Constitution and decided he could not help Marbury. Marshall concluded that:

- Marbury had become a judge when appointed and could not be deprived of his commission.
- Madison had violated the law in not delivering Marbury's commission.
- Congress had given the Supreme Court the power to force Madison to turn over the appointment when it passed an act authorizing the Supreme Court to issue writs necessary to make government officers do what was required of them.

Unfortunately for Marbury, Marshall found that the law Congress passed giving the Supreme Court original jurisdiction to issue the writ violated the Constitution. Congress did not have the power to give the Supreme Court the right to even listen to Marbury's case. The Constitution was very clear about the cases over which the Supreme Court had original jurisdiction and Marbury's case was not one of them, so the law under which Marbury sued was unconstitutional.

What section of Article III did the writ statute violate?

_____

Marshall had used the power of the Court to declare a law passed by Congress unconstitutional. Marbury never got to serve as a judge, but Marshall had made it clear that the Supreme Court had perhaps the most important power of all, the power to review laws passed by Congress. This review has come to be known as "judicial review."

Take Another Look

Checked and Balanced

The Supreme Court's role in judicial review of the laws Congress passes is an important part of the checks and balances provided for by the structure of the Constitution. It's a little like the game "paper, rock, scissors." There are three branches of the federal government: judicial, legislative, executive. No one of the three branches really gets the upper hand because each branch has ways to keep the others in control.

Here's a partial list of some of the important powers of each branch. Using these and other powers, make a chart that shows how the power of each branch is checked or balanced by a power held by another branch.

Judicial
can declare law
   unconstitutional
can declare an executive
   action unconstitutional

Legislative
passes laws
can override veto of law

Executive
can veto laws
appoints judges

Chasing Him Out

As powerful a tool as judicial review is for the Court, impeachment is a powerful tool over which Congress has authority. Early in the life of the Constitution, there was concern that impeachment would be used as a way to wield political power. The framers did not want this to happen, so they wrote that a person should be removed from office only for "treason, bribery, and other high crimes and misdemeanors."

Find out what happened in the impeachment case of Justice Chase and about the subsequent impeachment history of the Supreme Court justices. The impeachment entry in an encyclopedia is a good starting point for this research. Write a short summary of what you find through your research.

Being a Citizen

The Supreme Court is made up of nine justices. One serves as the chief justice. Find out the names of the nine justices who serve today. Find a newspaper or magazine article about one of these justices. Does the article give you any idea about how the justice feels about important issues that face the Court? Does the article shed light on how the justice views his or her role as a lawmaker? Consider these questions as you write a summary of the article.

ARTICLE IV
State to State

How the States Relate

The Constitution states that all states must respect the court decisions and the laws of other states.

- Read Article IV, Section I (page 77). This section uses the famous phrase "full faith and credit." In your own words, write what this means.

_____

- Read Article IV, Section II, Clause 2 (page 78). This clause relates to the "extradition" of persons charged with crimes. *Extradition* is the process by which fugitives must be returned to the state in which their crime was committed. If a person commits a crime in one state, he or she cannot escape punishment by fleeing to a different state. What can the governor of the state in which the crime was committed demand regarding a fugitive?

_____

The writers of the Constitution believed that the boundaries of the United States would continue to change, so the Constitution allows for this.

- Read Article IV, Section III, Clause 1 (page 78). Who has authority to admit new states to the union?

_____

If a new state is to be formed from part of a state or by joining two states, who must give consent?

_____

As the United States grew, new lands called *territories* came under its control.

- Read Article IV, Section III, Clause 2 (page 78). List the two powers Congress has over territories belonging to the United States.

_____

- Read Article IV, Section IV (page 78). What does the United States guarantee to every state, and what two things will it protect each state against?

_____

We the People, Copyright © Pamela A. Marx

Take Another Look

Fugitive Slaves

At the time the Constitution was written, there were many states that had economies which relied on slavery. To reach an agreement on a constitutional framework, those who opposed slavery compromised and allowed for its continued existence. Article IV, Section II, Clause 3, reflected the compromise of the time by requiring the return of escaped slaves to their owners, even if the slaves were caught in free states.

With the rise of the Underground Railroad in the 1800s—which helped runaway slaves escape to Canada—Southerners became dissatisfied with the language in the Constitution. They pushed Congress for stricter fugitive slave laws. There were fiery arguments in Congress about what, if any, law should be passed. The result of all this conflict was the Fugitive Slave Act of 1850. Research this act. Then divide into groups to role-play the parts of Northerners and Southerners. "Northerners" argue the Fugitive Slave Act from the northern perspective. "Southerners" argue the Fugitive Slave Act from the southern perspective.

Calling Out the Federal Troops

In 1894, President Grover Cleveland sent federal troops to Chicago during a strike of railroad workers, the Pullman Strike. In 1962, federal troops were sent to Mississippi when James Meredith, a black Air Force veteran, became the first black student to attend the University of Mississippi. Find out more about one of these incidents. Who requested that troops be sent?

Discuss your findings with the class. Debate whether or not the federal government was right to send in troops.

Being a Citizen

Imagine that you are an editorial writer for the local newspaper. A person accused of bombing a building in your city has fled to another state. The governor of your state has requested the return of this person for trial and the governor of the other state has refused, stating that the person should not be tried because he had a difficult childhood and is mentally ill. Write an editorial about whether this person should be extradited.

ARTICLES V AND VI
Amendments to the Constitution and Federal Supremacy

The writers of the Constitution created a document that was meant to work for generations. They realized that, for the Constitution to provide stability for the growing country years into the future, there had to be a way to change this document, or add to it, as the need arose. Yet, for the country to remain stable, a change or amendment had to be made thoughtfully—not easily, or on a whim. Article V sets out the procedures the writers agreed upon for amending the Constitution.

∽ Read Article V (page 78). One way to amend the Constitution is for Congress to propose an amendment. By what vote of which houses must a proposed amendment succeed to begin the process?

_____

Another way an amendment can be proposed is by a convention of the states. What portion of state legislatures must vote for a convention so it can be called?

_____

After an amendment is proposed, what portion of the legislatures or conventions in the states must ratify the amendment for it to become part of the Constitution?

_____

∽ Read Article VI, Clause 2 (page 79). The Constitution is part of the "supreme law of the land." What are the other two things that also make up this supreme law?

_____

The writers of the Constitution recognized that, while each state would have its own government and laws to manage state affairs, there could be no question that the *federal law* (national laws passed under the Constitution) would prevail if a conflict arose between state and federal laws. This division of government responsibilities between the federal government and state governments is called *federalism*.

We the People, Copyright © Pamela A. Marx

Take Another Look

Equal Rights Amendment

In the late 1970s and the early 1980s, an attempt was made to add an amendment to the Constitution. The amendment was called the Equal Rights Amendment ("ERA"). This amendment was an attempt to ensure "equality of rights under the law" so that no one would be discriminated against on the basis of his or her sex. Ultimately, the amendment was not ratified and did not become a part of the Constitution. Research the history of this proposed amendment.

Pretend it is 1980. Decide for yourself if the amendment should be ratified, and create a billboard advertisement designed to encourage people to call their state legislatures about the amendment. Will your billboard be in favor of ratification or opposed? Include some of your reasons on your billboard.

Prohibition and Its Repeal

The amendment procedures of Article V allow the Constitution to be flexible enough to make changes, and then undo those changes if they prove to be a mistake. In 1919, the Progressive Movement led to the adoption of the 18th Amendment, which prohibited the manufacture, distribution, and sale of alcoholic beverages. It quickly became clear that this measure caused more problems than it solved. Crime rose and the use of alcohol continued. A movement for repeal of prohibition gained steam.

Research the problems that prohibition caused. Then create a political advertisement urging Congress to repeal the 18th Amendment, or write and present a public service announcement for the radio. This announcement could state why it is important that prohibition be repealed quickly.

Being a Citizen

Can you think of ideas for a new amendment to the Constitution? As a class, brainstorm ideas for amendments. One student could list the ideas on the board. Then form smaller groups. Each group should choose one of the strongest ideas and write it up as an amendment. Use very clear language. Finally, meet as a class. Each group in turn should present its amendment and have the class discuss whether each amendment proposed should be ratified.

ARTICLE VII
Ratification of the Constitution

✍ Read the first sentence of Article VII (page 79). The writers agreed that less than unanimous consent would do to ratify the new Constitution. Out of the twelve states present, how many states were required to approve the Constitution for it to become effective?

_____

As the constitutional conventions met, the state of Massachusetts became very important. Massachusetts was at the time the second most populous state. If the Constitution failed to be ratified there, the ratification effort might fail completely. As the Constitution was discussed, one thing became clear. Many citizens were concerned about ratifying it because the new Constitution did not contain a clear statement of the rights of individuals. Those favoring its ratification promised that a bill of rights would be adopted when the first Congress met. With this assurance, Massachusetts ratified.

The Bill of Rights was adopted, and it contained the Ninth and Tenth Amendments.

✍ Read the Ninth Amendment (page 80). It says that the enumeration, or listing, of specific rights in the Bill of Rights cannot be interpreted to deny or limit the existence of other rights. Who holds these other rights?

_____

✍ Read the Tenth Amendment (page 80). This amendment turns its attention to the powers of the states as well as individuals. Many citizens in the late 1700s were afraid of a strong central government. They did not want to be told what to do by someone who lived far away. The Tenth Amendment helped address these concerns. It says that any powers not given to the federal government or specifically denied to the states are reserved. To whom are these powers reserved?

_____

Take Another Look

Countdown to Ratification

Article VII required that nine states had to ratify the Constitution before it could become effective. Research this time period, and create a timeline from the signing of the Constitution by George Washington and thirty-eight others to the adoption of the Bill of Rights by the first Congress. Include the order of ratification by the states.

Bill of Rights

The Bill of Rights is made up of the first 10 amendments to the Constitution. Form a small group. Pretend you are demanding a guarantee of the rights of individuals before you will support the Constitution. Having just dealt with many forms of English oppression, decide on five guarantees included in the first 10 amendments that you think would be most important to you and to others. In turn, talk about the five guarantees and why you chose them.

Being a Citizen

Sometimes these personal guarantees of freedom and personal rights seem like something distant and far away. Is the Bill of Rights important to you? Are individual rights still important today? Below is a list of some of the rights contained in the Bill of Rights. Choose one of them. Write a short essay explaining why and how it is important to you. Give examples of how you are or could be affected by this right in your daily life.

- You have religious freedom. The government cannot tell you what church you must attend. It cannot require you to attend church at all.

- You have the right to free speech. You can express your opinions, whether they be positive or negative, about the government, its schools, and the community in which you live without the government putting you in jail or fining you for your ideas.

- The government has a power to take property it needs for a public purpose, but you have rights too. The government cannot confiscate your property to use for a public purpose without first paying you a just amount. For example, in order to take your house from you to create a street or widen a highway, the government must pay you the fair value of your house.

The First Amendment

〜

Freedom of Religion

The First Amendment sets forth several very important personal guarantees. The first part of the amendment is about religious freedom. It is divided into two parts.

〜 Read the First Amendment (page 79). Who cannot make laws interfering with religious freedom?

_____

The writers said that there shall be ". . . no law respecting an establishment of religion." This is called the "establishment clause." What do you think it means to "establish" a religion?

_____

In the next phrase, the writers said that there could be no laws prohibiting the free exercise of religion. This is the "free exercise" clause.

The concept of what it means to "establish" a religion has developed over the years. The courts have decided that neither Congress nor the states can establish a religion by making one religion the official state religion. No governmental power can give one religious group preferred treatment. Neither can the government treat one religious group less favorably than another.

While people have the absolute right to believe without government interference, there can be some restrictions on the actions taken in the name of those beliefs. Restrictions on things we do as part of our religion can only be justified if the government can show a really important reason why. Two examples of the Court's rulings on religious issues follow.

• The Mormons practiced polygamy as part of their religious beliefs. This practice violated a law against bigamy. In 1879, the Court said that the law could restrict the Mormons. See _Reynolds_ v. _United States_ (page 68).

• In 1972, the Court allowed the Amish to keep their children out of school after the eighth grade, since the teachings in public high schools conflicted with their religion. The Court weighed the infringement on religion against the public interest served. See _Wisconsin_ v. _Yoder_ (page 69).

We the People, Copyright © Pamela A. Marx

Take Another Look

Many People, Many Religions

When the writers of the First Amendment wrote about free exercise of religion, they were drawing on lessons from their recent history. The first lesson—that without tolerance there could be no peace—came after years of fighting caused by religious intolerance after the Reformation in Europe. The second lesson—that people will go to great lengths and suffer tremendous personal losses to have religious freedom—came after the restrictions on worship that led the first colonists to come to America. The writers of the First Amendment also believed that people who did not practice any religion must have that freedom as well.

Interview someone who has a religious belief different from yours. Write a short summary of how his or her beliefs differ from yours.

What's "Establishment"?

Sometimes it can be hard to decide whether a law or governmental practice constitutes the "establishment" of religion. Debate the following.

- Your city puts up an annual winter holiday display. The display includes a manger scene, colored lights, Santa Claus, and a snowman. Does the inclusion of the manger have any nonreligious purpose? Does the display favor any religion? Would you feel differently if the display included a Hannukah menorah?

- The school district used to broadcast morning prayer over the loud-speaker. It has now replaced the prayer with a mandatory moment of silence. Does the current practice encourage religious practice? Is there a nonreligious reason for the moment of silence?

Compare your conclusions with those reached by the Supreme Court in *Lynch* v. *Donnelly* (page 67) and *Wallace* v. *Jaffree* (page 68).

Being a Citizen

Does being asked to learn about the theory of evolution violate the religious freedom of those who believe that God created the earth and its creatures (*creationism*)? Can a state require the teaching of creationism if it allows the teaching of evolution? The Supreme Court considered this issue. Read the summary of the Court's decision in *Edwards* v. *Aguillard* (page 66). Write a short essay on whether or not you agree with the Court's decision and why.

Freedom of Speech

The First Amendment states "Congress shall make no law . . . abridging the freedom of speech. . . ." Speech can take many forms. Make a list of different ways people can voice their opinions. Do not include books, newspapers, and other publications. (These will be discussed under the subject of a free press.) Think of at least five different ways people can express how they feel about an issue.

_____

_____

_____

_____

_____

The writers of the Constitution were most concerned about protecting people's rights to express their political opinions and ideas, but the Supreme Court has also protected nonpolitical speech, such as advertising. The First Amendment says there can be no law abridging freedom of speech, but does this mean that we are free to say anything we want? Consider the following kinds of speech. Should the First Amendment protect them?

- Mary Mouth testifies in court under oath that she saw Sam Slick grab and carry off her purse in a shopping mall. She does not like Sam and never clearly saw the person who snatched her bag in the crowded mall.

- Ted Talker wears a shirt to the grocery store that uses a vulgar term to tell the police what he thinks of them.

- Students at a public school stage a march protesting the principal's position on surprise weapons searches of students. They carry signs that read, "The principal has the IQ of a rock!" They shout, "No searches, no way!"

The First Amendment gives us the right to free speech. Why is free speech important to a democracy?

_____

_____

We the People, Copyright © Pamela A. Marx

Take Another Look

Many Kinds of Speech

Read the following case facts. Pretend that you are a judge and write a brief summary of your ruling.

It was the late 1960s, and United States troops were fighting in Vietnam. People of all ages disagreed with the United States' involvement. Three students in Iowa wanted to protest the war at their public school. They arrived at school wearing black arm bands as a symbol of protest. The principal sent them home.

Did the principal's action violate the students' free speech rights? To write your opinion, think about these things: In what ways were the arm bands a method of speech, and in what ways were they not? Could the arm bands help promote discussion between students on the war? Did arm bands disrupt school business? Was it reasonable for the principal to send students home because of a vague fear that the arm bands might cause disruption? After you have written your opinion, read *Tinker* v. *Des Moines School District* (page 68).

Being a Citizen

Survey five people outside your class on how they feel about the forms of speech listed below. Should they be allowed? If so, should the speaker face consequences?

Situation A A candidate for mayor tells local leaders that the current mayor never finished college and was arrested once for shoplifting. Neither statement is true.

Situation B A television advertisement for Amazacillin states that it will kill bacterial infections faster than other products with no side effects. The company that makes Amazacillin has studies showing that 25 percent of children who use the antibiotic develop severe headaches.

Situation C Protesters against the death penalty march outside the county courthouse yelling "Death is cruel and unusual punishment." They block the entrance to the courthouse, making it difficult for judges, lawyers, and witnesses to enter to do business.

Meet in groups to discuss the results of your surveys and brainstorm ways the speech can be modified in place, time, or method to be acceptable.

Freedom of the Press and Free Assembly

There are two important purposes of a free press. One is to make sure that the public is informed about all kinds of matters. The second is to operate as a check on the government and the activities of its officials, both elected and appointed. Because writers and editors of newspapers, books, and magazines have a right to express opinions and investigate and report both good and bad findings, it is not easy for officials to limit the information that is printed and read by the public.

Censorship of what is printed, distributed, and read is a threat to freedom of the press. What is censorship? Look up the word "censorship" in your dictionary. What does it mean to censor something?

_____

One way of censoring what people can read is to prevent something from being published in the first place. This is called a *prior restraint*. The Supreme Court closely watches cases of prior restraint because they are the most threatening to the First Amendment. Consider the following cases.

- A court order stops the press from reporting the movement of troops, equipment, and battle plans of the military during an armed conflict.

- A court order prohibits the press from reporting on certain subjects relating to a trial about a shocking multiple murder until the jury is selected. (See *Nebraska Press Association* v. *Stuart*, page 67).

Do these cases affect government interests in ways that justify a prior restraint? Explain.

_____

_____

The First Amendment protects the right of people to gather together, or "peaceably assemble," to discuss political ideas. Identify times and places in your community where people gather together to discuss political issues.

_____

The First Amendment also gives people the right to petition the government for "redress of grievances." What does this mean?

_____

We the People, Copyright © Pamela A. Marx

Take Another Look

Can the Library Do That?

Some books that have been censored in different places in the United States since their publication are *Huckleberry Finn* by Mark Twain, *In the Night Kitchen* (a picture book) by Maurice Sendak, and *To Kill a Mockingbird* by Harper Lee. A book may be censored as racist, sexist, sacrilegious, or immoral.

Read the children's book *In the Night Kitchen* by Maurice Sendak. Check its original publication date in the front of the book. At the time of publication, many parents were concerned about unacceptable frontal nudity in the artwork.

Divide into two debate groups. One group will play the role of parents who want the book removed from the school library. The other group will play the role of parents who find the book acceptable.

Being a Citizen

The year is 1983. The place is a high school in Missouri. Students on the newspaper have written two stories, one dealing with teen pregnancy and the other with the effects of divorce on children. The principal pulls the articles, and the paper is published without them. The student writers sue the school district. (See *Hazelwood School District* v. *Kuhlmeier,* page 66.)

This is a classic case of *prior restraint,* but it happened on a school newspaper. The students writing the articles were members of the newspaper class. The Supreme Court decided that the newspaper was a learning program, which the school officials had the right to control. This control allowed them to censor articles. Pretend you are a justice on the Supreme Court. Write your own opinion. Do you agree or disagree with the court? To decide, consider these facts:

- The newspaper is a class publication supported by taxpayer dollars.
- The identities of the divorced parents mentioned in the article were divulged and the parents had no opportunity to respond.
- The teen pregnancy article made sexual references not appropriate to the age level of the students.

The Second and Third Amendments

The Right to Bear Arms and More

The Second Amendment is a simple sentence. It may be short, but it has inspired great debate in recent years. Just what does the Second Amendment say?

"A well-regulated Militia, being necessary to the security of a free State, the right of the people to keep and bear Arms, shall not be infringed."

In order to interpret this amendment, it is important to know the meaning of all of its words. Define the following words:

militia _____

security _____

arms _____

What reason does the amendment give for the people's right to keep arms?

_____

Could the word *people* mean several different things? Does it mean "individuals"? Could it mean "the states and their citizens"? Or could it mean some other governmental framework that represents the people, such as cities or counties? What do you think?

_____

_____

_____

In order to have a militia available to assist in keeping the nation free, do people need to have the right to keep guns in their homes? Why? Why not?

_____

_____

The Third Amendment protects people against the use of their homes by soldiers. It states that this cannot be done in wartime without the government following certain rules. Can it be done at all in peacetime, and, if so, how?

_____

_____

We the People, Copyright © Pamela A. Marx

Take Another Look

Restrictions on the Right to Bear Arms

There are many kinds of laws in effect about gun ownership. Guns must be registered. Gun sellers must be licensed. There can be waiting periods imposed before purchasers receive their guns.

Find out what kinds of laws there are in your state that limit the ownership of guns. To research this, call your local city council person or the mayor's office to begin your investigation. Do you think the restrictions you found are reasonable? Do you think they are sufficient? Summarize your findings and feelings on the issue.

A Soldier in Your Home?

There were only ten amendments in the Bill of Rights, and one of these is about the quartering of soldiers in houses without the owner's consent. Today this right may not seem as important as rights to free speech and against self-incrimination, but in the 18th century, the issue was fresh on people's minds. In 1763, less than a month after the British passed the infamous Stamp Act, the Quartering Act of 1763 was put in place. Frustrated colonists were faced with a law ordering that, if there were not enough barracks available to house British troops, taverns, inns, and even private homes could be used to house them. While the owner was entitled to some payment, the prospect of being ordered to host a soldier angered the colonists.

Time travel back to the 1760s. Work in groups to create skits that demonstrate how the colonists' privacy and property rights were violated by such a law. Perform your skits for the class.

Being a Citizen

Groups against gun control, including the National Rifle Association, support the individual's right to own and use guns. They emphasize the role of guns in sports, such as hunting, as well as for personal protection. Groups in favor of gun control emphasize the dangers from the sale of automatic weapons and small handguns and point out the resultant street crime and home accidents.

Divide into groups and research positions for and against gun control. As a group, choose a side and then debate a group with the opposing viewpoint.

The Fourth Amendment

Search, Seizures, and Probable Cause

The Fourth Amendment protects us from being arrested and searched without reason, both in our homes and as we go about the business of our daily lives.

∽ Read the Fourth Amendment (page 79).

The Constitution helps to insure that searches and seizures are reasonable by requiring the police to obtain warrants before searching a place or arresting people on the suspicion of having committed a crime. There are two types of warrants: warrants to search a person or premises and warrants to arrest a person. The Fourth Amendment also states that warrants can only be issued upon a certain type of finding, supported by oath or affirmation. What must the police show in order to obtain a warrant?

_____

What are two things that the Fourth Amendment states the warrant must describe specifically?

_____

_____

As you might imagine, what constitutes "probable cause" for a judge or public official to issue a warrant has been debated before the Supreme Court through the years. However, the Court has found some general rules that may be applied. Generally, to obtain a search warrant, the requesting police officers must show enough facts to prove that it is probable (more than 50 percent likely) that the items sought are connected with a crime and that they will be found in the place the police want to search. To obtain an arrest warrant, facts must show that it is probable that a crime has been committed and that the person to be arrested committed it.

When a search warrant is issued, the Fourth Amendment states that the premises to be searched must be "particularly described." What do you think this means? Why is it important for this information to be specific? Is an address enough? What if the address is an apartment building?

_____

_____

We the People, Copyright © Pamela A. Marx

Take Another Look

Our Informant Says

When the only fact supporting a request for a search warrant was that a credible informant had said that narcotics were concealed at a certain location, the warrant was denied. The Supreme Court agreed that this was not enough evidence to justify the warrant. (See *Aguilar* v. *Texas*, page 66.) Listed below are questions the justices might have asked. Rank them in order of their importance in determining if there is "probable cause" to issue a warrant. Then justify your ranking.

- Did the informant give police officers information in the past that had proved accurate? What kind of citizen was he? A police officer? A crime victim? A criminal?

- Why did the informant think drugs were on the premises?

- Did the informant know about the drugs because someone else told him that there were drugs there? Was this information reliable?

- Did the informant think drugs were on the premises because he observed someone acting suspiciously there?

Being a Citizen

Not all searches or arrests must be preceded by a warrant. Think about these situations:

- A woman shoplifted expensive perfume from a department store, and the theft was caught on store surveillance cameras. The store notified the police and stated that it had the videotape evidence of the theft. The police went to the woman's home without first obtaining a warrant.

- As a police car patrolled the street in front of a liquor store, officers heard shots fired, saw the clerk fall behind the counter, and observed two men and a woman run out of the store. The police called for an ambulance and pursued the threesome. They handcuffed and arrested them.

Pretend you are the district attorney. Consider the seriousness of the crimes, the evidence the police had, the likelihood of escape of the suspects, and the potential danger to others. Decide if you think these warrantless arrests would be seen as constitutional by a jury.

The Fifth Amendment

Double Jeopardy, Self-Incrimination, and More

This first part of the Fifth Amendment deals with very serious crimes. Look up the definition of the adjective *capital* in the dictionary. Describe in your own words what a *capital crime* is.

_____

     Read the Fifth Amendment (page 80).

What has to have occurred before a person can be held for a capital crime?

_____

An *indictment* is a formal charge against a person accusing him or her of a crime. The indictment is issued by a *grand jury,* which is a group of citizens that reviews the evidence against an accused person. If a majority agrees that there is enough evidence against the accused, the person is held for trial.

Putting a person on trial for the same crime more than once is called *double jeopardy.* If a person were tried for a crime and found innocent, and then the police found more evidence and wanted to put the person on trial again for the same crime, that would be subjecting the person to double jeopardy. What language does the amendment use to describe double jeopardy?

_____

Perhaps in television courtroom scenes you have heard a witness say, "I refuse to answer on the grounds that it might tend to incriminate me." What does he or she mean by that?

_____

_____

From the time an individual is arrested or in police custody and not free to go, his or her Fifth Amendment rights become active. The arresting authorities must advise the person of his or her right not to answer questions. Why do you think it is important for authorities to remind the suspect of this right?

_____

_____

We the People, Copyright © Pamela A. Marx

Take Another Look

Miranda Rights

In 1966, the Supreme Court decided a case that many people thought dramatically expanded the right against self-incrimination. For years, there had been many questions about when confessions of an accused person could be used against him or her at trial. If used in court, the accused was effectively testifying against himself or herself. Therefore, to be used, the confession had to be voluntary. Many confessions were, and are, obtained after a person is arrested, but before trial. This raised questions about the tactics the police might use to obtain confessions from arrested persons— were the confessions really voluntary? In the case of *Miranda* v. *Arizona*, the court set out standards for determining if a confession is given by a person who knowingly and voluntarily waives his or her Fifth Amendment rights.

Research what the Miranda rights are. Do you think police take them seriously today? How can you find out?

Being a Citizen

The hearings of the House Un-American Activities Committee in the 1950s were led by Senator Joseph McCarthy. Many people were called to give testimony at these hearings about whether individuals they knew were members of the Communist Party. The pressure on witnesses to name names was tremendous. Some people named names while others "took the Fifth," meaning they refused to testify on the grounds they might incriminate themselves. These hearings gave rise to the blacklist. When someone was *blacklisted,* his or her name was added to a list of people who were accused of being Communists or Communist sympathizers. These people found it very hard to find jobs.

Work in small groups to research these hearings. Then create skits enacting hearing scenes. Have one student play Senator McCarthy while others play various roles of people giving testimony, either "naming names" or "taking the Fifth."

The Sixth Amendment

Our Rights in a Criminal Trial

The Sixth Amendment sets out many important rights to which people accused of a crime are entitled during their trials. The sentence for some crimes is time in jail or prison, or a fine. Each of these losses is considered a serious infringement of personal liberty. Since a criminal trial places personal rights in jeopardy, important rights are granted to the accused to assure the fairness of the trial itself and the sentence imposed.

Read the Sixth Amendment (page 80). The amendment uses two words to describe the type of trial to which an accused has a right—speedy and public. Why are they important to the accused?

_____

_____

Who decides whether the accused is guilty or innocent, and from where must these people be chosen?

_____

The amendment provides four more safeguards to the fair and just trial of an accused. Of what does the accused have a right to be informed?

_____

Which persons must he or she be able to confront as the trial proceeds?

_____

Which persons does he or she have the right to demand appear at the trial on his or her behalf?

_____

A compulsory process called *subpoena* is used to demand the appearance of these persons if they do not want to appear.

From whom does he or she have the right to obtain assistance?

_____

Take Another Look

An Impartial Jury

Read the play "12 Angry Men," by Reginald Rose, or watch the movie directed by Sidney Lumet. Consider the different kinds of people who were members of the jury. Not one of them was without individual prejudices, but together they found a new way to look at the issues.

Write a review of the play or movie. Describe how the story demonstrates the importance and/or problems of the jury system in ensuring a fair trial.

A Public Trial and the Right to Call Witnesses

Read *The Ox-Bow Incident* by Walter Van Tilberg Clark, or watch the movie directed by William Wellman. In it a group of citizens form a posse to find the perpetrators of a crime and then hold a hillside trial. Make a list of the ways in which this vigilante justice violates the Sixth Amendment.

Being a Citizen

It was not until 1963 that the Supreme Court decided that an accused person had a right to counsel, even if he could not pay for it himself, in all criminal cases. Clarence Earl Gideon was the man who helped the Supreme Court change its mind. Before Gideon's case, the Court had said that only in cases in which the death penalty was threatened was there a right to appointed counsel if the defendant could not afford to pay for his own (see *Betts* v. *Brady,* page 66). This case was overruled by the case Gideon brought. Gideon was no model citizen. He had been in and out of jail his whole life, but he believed the Constitution meant what it said about the right to counsel. (See *Gideon* v. *Wainwright,* page 66.) Find out more about the Gideon case. Write a summary on either Gideon's life or the Court's decision in *Gideon* v. *Wainwright.*

An excellent resource is the book *Gideon's Trumpet* by Anthony Lewis (Random House, 1966).

The Seventh and Eighth Amendments

More About the Court System

These two amendments provide individuals with more rights if and when they become involved with the court systems of this country. Because the Eighth Amendment is specifically concerned with rights in the criminal justice system, we will look at that amendment first.

∽ Read the Eighth Amendment (page 80). *Bail* is an amount of money an accused person is required to give to the court if he or she is to be free pending a trial. Bail is often arranged through a person called a *bail bondsman*. What does the amendment say about the amount of bail?

_____

When the charge is a very serious crime, such as violent assault or murder, the judge may decide that, regardless of the level of bail required, the person might flee the court's jurisdiction. In such a case, the judge might deny bail altogether.

The Eighth Amendment speaks to the punishment imposed upon a person if convicted of a crime. *Fines* are amounts of money a person is required to pay as punishment for conviction of a crime. What does the amendment say about fines?

_____

Besides fines, what other kinds of punishment can you think of that a court could order against someone convicted of a crime?

_____

What kinds of punishments cannot be inflicted?

_____

∽ Read the Seventh Amendment (page 80). The Seventh Amendment talks about court cases that are not criminal. These are called *suits at common law.* For any dispute involving more than a certain amount of money, to what does the amendment say a person has a right?

_____

Take Another Look

Breach of Contract Cases

Cases involving disagreements over contracts are called *breach of contract cases*. Much of the buying and selling of goods between two people or companies is done by contract. In a contract, each person agrees to do something. When there is a contract, each party has certain rights and certain responsibilities. You probably have informal contracts with people right now. Your agreement to do chores for allowance is a kind of contract. Your agreement to babysit for someone is a kind of contract.

In a good contract, the rights and responsibilities are balanced. Each side gives up something, and each side gets a benefit. Write a list of your rights and responsibilities in some of the contractlike arrangements you have with people. Then, write a contract to cover one of those arrangements. Identify the parties to the contract, what each party is supposed to do, and when and where the tasks will be done. Leave a place for both parties to sign.

All Kinds of Cases

Become aware of the law at work around you by reading your local newspaper or weekly news magazines. Often these publications have a section on recent developments in the law or important court cases. Find articles about at least three different cases. Decide whether each is a civil or a criminal case.

Being a Citizen

An often-debated topic is whether any form of capital punishment for any crime is constitutional under the Eighth Amendment. Capital punishment is putting someone to death for the crime committed. One of the complaints about capital punishment is that too often it is the poor defendant who is a member of a minority group who receives such a sentence. In some states, capital punishment had been entirely abolished, only to be reinstated again at a later date. Divide into groups. Research and debate whether capital punishment violates the Eighth Amendment.

The 14th and 15th Amendments

After the Civil War: Equal Protection and Due Process

The 14th Amendment affects many aspects of life in the United States.

෴ Read Section 1 of the 14th Amendment (page 81). What persons are citizens of the United States and the state in which they live?

_____

The section goes on to restrict the states from engaging in certain activities. What kinds of laws are the states prevented from making or enforcing?

_____

Due process of law can be described as a set of fair procedures. What are three things that no state can deprive any person of without due process of law?

_____

The 14th Amendment made it clear that the rights in the Bill of Rights were protected, not only against restrictions from the United States government, but also against restrictions imposed by the governments of the individual states.

෴ Read Section 2 of the 14th Amendment (page 81). This section stopped short of guaranteeing what right of citizenship to former slaves?

_____

෴ Read Sections 3, 4, and 5 of the 14th Amendment (page 82). Who could not hold public office under Section 3?

_____

What debts and claims were neither the United States nor any individual state allowed to pay?

_____

෴ Read the 15th Amendment (page 82). What right of citizenship did this amendment make clear that all citizens of this country have?

_____

Take Another Look

The Civil War Ends, but Questions Remain

Divide into groups to create skits in which students play the roles of the writers of Sections 3 and 4 of the 14th Amendment. In the skits, recreate the arguments and discussions that might have occurred in the writing of these two sections. Some actors should be working toward the goal of reunifying southern states. Others should play the role of those who sought to punish Southerners for the war.

The Equal Protection Clause

Though slavery was abolished by the 13th Amendment, former slaves continued to suffer unfair, discriminatory treatment. The 14th Amendment was an effort to end discrimination. Specifically, the "equal protection" language stated that the laws of the land must be enforced to insure their equal application to and protection of all people, regardless of race.

Research one of the following cases. Write an editorial about the decision and the ways in which it failed to provide for equal protection.

- *Plessy* v. *Ferguson.* In 1896, a Louisiana state law required that there be separate railroad cars for black and white passengers. This law was challenged and the Court found that it was constitutional because it provided for "separate, but equal" facilities for each race. This decision was used to justify all separate facilities for blacks and whites—including separate, segregated schools.

- *Korematsu* v. *United States.* In 1942, Japanese-American citizens and persons of Japanese heritage living on the West Coast were detained by presidential order in internment camps, without hearings or accusations of a crime. The public feared that these people might sabotage the war effort with Japan. The unfairness of this order was argued before the Court. The Court found that this treatment based upon race did *not* violate the equal protection clause and that sometimes public necessity could justify such treatment. No Germans or Italians were detained in this way even though the country was also at war with Germany and Italy.

Being a Citizen

Put yourself in the position of a Japanese farmer who is being detained in 1942. Review the Bill of Rights and identify all the rights you are being denied. Write a letter to President Roosevelt outlining the constitutional rights you have lost as a result of his emergency detention order.

The 19th, 23rd, 24th, and 26th Amendments

More Voting Rights After the 15th Amendment

Each of these amendments affected voting rights in this country.

✍ Read the 19th Amendment (page 83). What fact about a person could no longer be used to exclude that person from exercising the right to vote?

_____

The 26th Amendment gives the right to vote to a different segment of the population based on age. Before the 26th Amendment was ratified, a person had to be to 21 years old in order to exercise the right to vote.

✍ Read the 24th Amendment (page 84). For many years, in some parts of the country, a person had to pay poll or other taxes before he or she could vote. This made it very hard for poor people to vote. In many of these places, many of the poor were black. This amendment outlawed poll taxes in elections of what officials?

_____

_____

The 23rd Amendment is different from the other amendments above in the voting rights it grants. The rights it grants are limited to the residents of a particular city within the United States.

✍ Read the 23rd Amendment, Section 1 (page 84). This amendment gives residents of the district that is the seat of government of the United States a way to participate in presidential elections. They did not have this right before because they were not residents of any state.

What city is the seat of the government of the United States?

_____

How many electors do the residents of this city send to the Electoral College?

_____

Take Another Look

Seneca Falls, New York—1848

The women's suffrage, or voting rights, movement began years before the 19th Amendment was finally passed by Congress. A women's rights convention was held in Seneca Falls, New York, in 1848. Some well-known female leaders of the past were: Elizabeth Cady Stanton, women's rights leader; Lucretia Mott, women's rights leader; Susan B. Anthony, women's voting rights leader; Elizabeth Blackwell, the first female medical school graduate; Lucy Stone, famed for retaining her maiden name after marriage; and Amelia Bloomer, famed for challenging fashion by wearing Turkish-style trousers. Pretend you are a creative consultant to an educational video company. Write a five- to eight-scene storyboard of the life of one of these leaders that could be used as the basis for an educational video.

War and the Vote

In the 1960s, many young men were being drafted into military service and sent to fight in the Vietnam War. Some people viewed the war as a valid fight against the encroachment of Communism around the world. Others thought the United States shouldn't interfere in another country's civil war. What became clear to many, however, was that, if an 18-year-old was old enough to be sent into battle, he was old enough to vote. So the movement to lower the voting age from 21 to 18 began.

Find out about this movement, the controversies of the time that generated it, and when the 26th Amendment was passed and ratified. Place yourself in the time of the Vietnam War as a young man who has been drafted (women were not subject to the draft). Write a letter to your representative or senator explaining why you think the 26th Amendment should be passed by Congress.

Being a Citizen

Place yourself in the position of a Washington, D.C. resident. The seat of the United States government resides in the city in which you live, yet the Constitution allows you to have only one nonvoting member of the House of Representatives. The 23rd Amendment gave you a way to participate in the presidential election, but you are still not represented in the House of Representatives or the Senate as you would be if you resided in a state instead of the district. How would you feel about this system? Do you think it is fair? Jot down in two columns reasons for and against this system.

You Be the Judge

The Interrupted Lesson

Just the Facts

Each day for a week, the students in Room 30 at Middlebrook School were interrupted during their math class by a sound truck parked across the street from the school. The sound truck's message about the need to repair school buildings so that they can better withstand earthquakes was repeated once every two minutes, so that anyone passing by would hear it.

While some of the Room 30 students enjoyed the interruption, others said the repeated blaring of the message made it impossible for them to concentrate on their work.

Soon parents contacted the local police. Local residents who lived near the truck also contacted the police. A day or so after the police were contacted, the man operating the truck was arrested for violating a city ordinance. The ordinance stated that "persons can make no loud or raucous noise in residential neighborhoods." The sound truck operator was fined under the city ordinance. He appealed his case which has now reached the Supreme Court.

What does the district attorney say?

- The ordinance is not designed to limit any particular content or information a speaker wants to express. Therefore, the ordinance is not an attempt to control the content of any speaker's words.
- The speaker's use of a sound truck interfered with the school's duty to educate and the students' right to learn.
- The speaker's use of a sound truck interfered with private residents' peaceful enjoyment of their homes and privacy. The residents have privacy rights under the Ninth Amendment, and the sound truck operator violated those rights.
- The police have historically not enforced the ordinance to restrict only certain kinds of speakers. The police have responded to *all* complaints of unreasonable noise.

What does the sound truck owner say?

- He has a First Amendment right to express his opinions.
- Nobody is suffering any physical injury from his method of speech, and he is not trying to incite anyone to any harmful or violent acts by his words.
- He needs to express his opinion near the school for it to have the impact it should.
- No other method of delivery will allow him to reach as many people who may be concerned about the issue as those who travel to, from, and near the school.
- By prohibiting "loud and raucous" speech, the ordinance allows police the discretion to interpret what is loud and raucous. They might interpret "loud and raucous" in such a way as to limit only certain kinds of content.

WHAT DO YOU THINK?

The case is before you at the Supreme Court. Decide whether the city ordinance violates the sound truck operator's First Amendment rights. Examine the arguments of each side. Write a brief opinion justifying your point of view. Make your decision by balancing the needs of the speaker and the importance of his First Amendment rights against the needs of the city to keep the peace and to provide a quiet educational environment.

After you have written your opinion, review *Kovacs* v. *Cooper* (page 67) to read the Court's decision in a similar case.

You Be the Judge

You Be the Judge

Nobody's Using Room B-12

Just the Facts

City School is a large, urban school with many special interest groups and activities. Most of the school clubs meet once a week during the lunch hour, in empty rooms at the school. There is a computer club, school spirit club, drama club, and service club. A new club called the prayer club wanted to start holding meetings during lunch hours, too. The club organizer, Chandra Channing, had lined up a teacher to supervise and identified an empty room—room B-12. Chandra asked the principal for permission for her club to meet. He said he would get back to her.

The principal thought about Chandra's proposal. He was concerned that, if he authorized a prayer club to meet, he would run into First Amendment problems with parents and community members who believe that the school has no authority to use tax-funded public school facilities to support or encourage religious behavior by students. The principal rejected Chandra's request, and she took her case to court. She lost at the trial and has appealed her case to the Supreme Court.

We the People, Copyright © Pamela A. Marx

What does the principal say?

- To allow a religious group to meet on campus is like establishing a church on campus. This would violate the First Amendment establishment clause that states that the government cannot establish religion.

- There is no nonreligious purpose for the club, which is designed for worship and prayer meetings.

- To give the club a room on campus to hold its meetings creates an entanglement between the school (as the government) and a particular religion. What if more and more religious groups seek space on campus? The school cannot accommodate an endless number of religious groups.

What does the student say?

- If the administration allows one club to meet, it must allow others to meet; it cannot pick and choose which clubs it will let use school facilities. To do so infringes upon the rights to free assembly, free speech, and free exercise of religion of those who would like to be involved in the prayer club.

- The prayer club is not forcing anyone to participate in the club or to practice religion on school property. The club is open to anyone who wants to come, but students are not pressured to join or attend. Thus, the school is not establishing a religion by allowing the club to meet.

- There is a nonreligious or secular purpose for allowing the club to meet— that is, it is a forum for the exchange of ideas.

- If nonreligious groups can use school facilities, the benefit to religion conferred by giving the club space to meet is incidental. The primary effect of giving the club space to meet is not of advancing a particular religion, but in allowing students having different interests to share their ideas.

WHAT DO YOU THINK?

This case is before you at the Supreme Court. Decide whether the principal's decision was a valid effort to avoid "establishing a religion" on campus or whether it was a violation of the students' rights of free speech and free exercise of religion. Look at the arguments of each side. Write an opinion justifying your point of view. To reach your decision, balance the interests raised by each side.

After you have written your opinion, review *Widmar* v. *Vincent* (page 69) to read the Court's decision in a similar case.

You Be the Judge

If You Want to Play Sports, You've Got to Play Ball

Just the Facts

Smith School District was experiencing a problem with drug use on its high school campus. Many of the high school athletes were using drugs. The district passed a rule that all athletes, in order to participate in sports, had to submit to mandatory drug testing at the beginning of the season and random drug testing during the season. Under the drug testing program, ten percent of all team members, male and female, were randomly chosen and tested each week. Same sex monitors insured that the samples were legitimately collected, but they engaged in their duties in a way that caused a minimum of intrusion on personal privacy.

Sara Softball, a female athlete, complained that the requirement of random testing without a reasonable suspicion of drug use was a violation of her Fourth Amendment rights against unreasonable searches. She took the case to court and lost. She has appealed the case to the Supreme Court.

What does the school district say?

- Students by law must attend school, and public schools have an obligation to provide a safe environment for all students. Special needs of school administrators to provide supervision of students means that students on campus cannot have the same expectation of privacy as a person walking down the street. The administrators' duty to provide a drug-free school makes the obtaining of warrants upon probable cause before drug testing impractical.
- Athletes give implied consent to a lower standard of privacy by agreeing to play sports. To play, they have to submit to a physical exam and dress in community locker rooms. Drug testing is a small added intrusion.
- The school has a legitimate interest in ensuring that its athletes are drug-free because drugs are physically dangerous. They lower coordination abilities and increase reaction times.

What does the student say?

- All students are compelled by law to attend school. If going to school is mandatory, students cannot be expected to give up their constitutional rights when they enter the school grounds. Requiring a student to give a urine test is a violation of privacy rights under the Fourth Amendment and the Ninth Amendment. It is a warrantless search of a person's body.
- When a student agrees to be an athlete, the student has not agreed to be treated with a lower standard of respect for privacy. Rather, the participation in sports benefits the school and improves the quality of the school environment. If a urine test is to be required, it should only be required if there is reasonable suspicion that the person is using drugs. There are observable standards such as reduced coordination, pupil dilation, and so on that could be used to justify requiring a drug test.

WHAT DO YOU THINK?

This case is before you at the Supreme Court. Decide whether the district's testing policy violates students' Fourth Amendment rights. Write an opinion for your point of view. Decide by balancing the students' privacy rights against the district's duty to provide safe, drug-free schools.

After you have written your opinion, review *Vernonia School District* v. *Acton* (page 68) to read the Court's decision in a similar case.

You Be the Judge

A Guide to Cited Cases

All references to "the Court" refer to the Supreme Court.

Aguilar v. Texas, 378 U.S. 108 (1964). Law enforcement officials asked for a search warrant with a written request stating that a credible informant had reported illegal drugs were hidden at a certain location. The Court said this was not enough. There needed to be a showing of why the informant was a believable witness and some facts about why the witness thought there were drugs on the premises.

Betts v. Brady, 316 U.S. 455 (1942). A poor man on trial for robbery requested that an attorney be appointed to represent him. His request was denied because local court practice permitted such appointment only in rape and murder cases. The Supreme Court upheld the local court practice. It said that the due process clause of the 14th Amendment did not require defendants to receive attorneys in all state criminal cases, but only in cases in which the circumstances of the case indicated that the failure to have an attorney would result in a trial lacking "fundamental fairness." See *Gideon* v. *Wainwright* for later developments.

Brown v. Board of Education I, 347 U.S. 483 (1954). A school district operated segregated schools. Blacks went to all black schools. Whites went to all white schools. The Court found this unconstitutional under the equal protection clause of the 14th Amendment. The Court ruled that separate educational facilities for children were "inherently unequal." The Court held this to be true even if the facilities and other aspects of the educational process are the same because enforced separation of the races reinforces a sense of inferiority.

Edwards v. Aguillard, 482 U.S. 578 (1987). Louisiana passed a law that required "balanced treatment" in public schools of the two theories of creation and evolution if the subject of human origins was taught. Both theories were defined as science and, while neither had to be taught, if one was taught the other had to be as well. The Court found the law unconstitutional. This law had no nonreligious purpose.

Gideon v. Wainwright, 372 U.S. 335 (1963). Gideon, a man who had been in and out of prison all his life, appealed in a handwritten document directly to the Court from jail. He claimed that his imprisonment as the result of a trial at which he was denied appointment of an attorney was a violation of his Sixth Amendment right to appointed counsel and that the Sixth Amendment applied to state cases because of the due process clause of the 14th Amendment. The Court agreed.

Hazelwood School District v. Kuhlmeier, 484 U.S. 260 (1988). A principal doing his usual review of the page proofs of the student newspaper censored two articles. The paper was published without the two articles. The students claimed the school had violated their rights to free speech. On appeal, the Court said that teachers may censor articles so long as the action is responsibly related to legitimate teaching goals. The students' rights were not violated.

Katzenburg v. McClung, 379 U.S. 294 (1964). McClung owned a restaurant called Ollie's Barbeque. The Civil Rights Act of 1964 ("CRA") prohibited racial discrimination in establishments engaged in selling food for consumption on the premises if the establishment served or offered to serve interstate travelers or a substantial part of the food served had moved in interstate commerce. Congress had based its right to regulate discrimination in local restaurants on its commerce clause power. McClung argued that the CRA did not apply to his facility since it served few interstate travelers and only a small part of the food it served customers each year had moved in interstate commerce before landing at Ollie's. The Court disagreed and said the CRA could regulate discriminatory behavior because the cumulative affect of many restaurants engaging in discrimination would affect interstate commerce.

***Korematsu* v. *United States*,** 323 U.S. 214 (1944). After the Japanese bombed Pearl Harbor, persons of Japanese heritage living on the West Coast, including Japanese-American citizens, were forced to evacuate their homes and relocate to detention camps. This was done by executive order of the president, as an emergency order due to the war with Japan. The people detained were given no hearing and no compensation for the property they lost. The Court upheld the executive order because of the wartime emergency the nation faced. Since that time, the Court's interpretation of the equal protection clause of the 14th Amendment has developed to make such a result unlikely today.

***Kovacs* v. *Cooper*,** 336 U.S. 77 (1949). A city ordinance stated that sound trucks could operate on public streets but could not amplify sounds to loud and raucous levels. A sound operator claimed this violated his First Amendment right to be heard. The Court upheld the ordinance. It said the state could protect the privacy of individuals by this law, since an unwilling listener had no other way of protecting himself or herself.

***Lynch* v. *Donnelly*,** 465 U.S. 668 (1984). The city of Pawtucket, Rhode Island, erected an annual Christmas display that included lights, a Santa, and a nativity scene. Citizens brought suit to have the nativity part of the display removed.

The Court stated the nativity scene was permissible because it explained the history of the holiday; thus, it was included for a non-religious reason. This display did not "establish" a religion.

***Marbury* v. *Madison*,** 5 U.S. 137 (1803). See discussion under "The Power of Judicial Review, " page 32.

***McCulloch* v. *Maryland*,** 17 U.S. 316 (1819). The national bank created by Congress was unpopular with the states, so Maryland passed a law taxing the bank. When the bank refused to pay the tax, Maryland sued. The Court found that the creation of the bank by Congress was an act necessary and proper to its express powers, such as the power to collect taxes and borrow money.

***Miranda* v. *Arizona*,** 384 U.S. 436 (1966). A poor man with mental health problems was arrested and taken to a special police room for questioning, where he confessed. He appealed his conviction claiming that his Fifth Amendment right not to incriminate himself had been violated. He had not been informed of his right to remain silent. The Court decided that the Fifth Amendment privilege against self-incrimination applies during the time an accused is being interrogated while in custody. "In custody" means when an individual is formally under arrest at a police station and also when he or she is deprived of his or her freedom of action in any significant way.

***Nebraska Press Association* v. *Stuart*,** 427 U.S. 539 (1976). To avoid dangers of pretrial publicity that would affect the fairness of an accused's trial in a multiple murder case, the judge entered an order. This order restricted the press from reporting certain subjects relating to the trial until after the jury was impaneled. The Court held this was an unnecessary prior restraint because the judge could insure a fair trial in other ways, such as changing the location of the trial.

A Guide to Cited Cases

Plessy v. *Ferguson,* 163 U.S. 537 (1896). Plessy was arrested for refusing to leave a whites only railroad car. Louisiana had a state law that required railroads to provide "equal but separate accommodations for the white and colored races." Plessy argued that the application of the law caused blacks to feel inferior, so it was unconstitutional, and that the equal protection provision of the 14th Amendment required that the law be struck down so that blacks and whites could be fairly treated by the railroads. The Court disagreed finding that equal protection was given by the requirement of separate but equal facilities. See *Brown* v. *Board of Education I* for later developments.

Reynolds v. *United States,* 98 U.S. 145 (1879). The Mormons practiced polygamy in the exercise of their religious beliefs. They believed it was a religious duty. A federal law prohibited bigamy. When the law was challenged because officials applied it to Mormons practicing polygamy, the Court held that Congress could forbid polygamy by law. It found governmental interests justifying such a law and stated that to give the Mormons special privileges to violate it would be giving a preference to one religion.

Shuttlesworth v. *City of Birmingham,* 394 U.S. 147 (1969). A city ordinance gave local officials power to grant parade permits. When reviewing requests, the ordinance allowed them to consider the effect the parade would have on the welfare and morals of the community. The Court held that this ordinance was unconstitutional "on its face." This means that, without even looking at the facts of how the licensing officials exercised their power, the ordinance's language showed it to be unconstitutional because there were no adequate standards built into the statute to assure its fair application to all.

Tinker v. *Des Moines School District,* 393 U.S. 503 (1969). Three students wore black arm bands to school to protest the Vietnam War. They did this despite a school policy prohibiting such behavior. The Court decided that the school could not ban and punish silent expression of opinion such as wearing arm bands. The arm band was a symbolic act that was a form of speech. While school officials can control conduct within school gates, students do not lose all their constitutional rights when they enter the school yard. The speech in question was silent, resulting in no disruption of school business. To prohibit a particular form of expression would only be justified upon a showing of material interference with school discipline.

United States v. *Eichman,* 496 U.S. 310 (1990). Due to many citizens' dislike of flag mutilation and burning as a form of symbolic speech, Congress passed a law against it. The law was challenged as a violation of First Amendment free speech rights. The Court found the law unconstitutional because the government cannot prohibit the expression of an idea as embodied in the act of flag burning, even if the purpose of the law is to preserve the flag as a symbol of national unity.

Vernonia School District v. *Acton,* 515 U.S. 646 (1995). A school district adopted a rule requiring students who participated in sports to agree to random drug testing. The rule was adopted because of a student drug abuse problem that involved many athletes. The Court found that the rule did not violate the unreasonable search provision of the Fourth Amendment because it was very specifically written and the district had an obligation to its students to maintain a safe school environment. Athletes taking drugs subjected both themselves and others to danger on the playing field and presented a bad example to others on campus who tended to see them as leaders. The school administered the testing in as limited and nonintrusive a way as possible to limit embarrassment while assuring accurate test results.

Wallace v. *Jaffree,* 472 U.S. 38 (1985). A law provided that public schools set aside a time of silence for meditation or voluntary prayer. The law was challenged as a violation of the establishment clause. The court held that the law was a violation of the "establishment clause" because both its text and its legislative history made clear that its sole purpose was to encourage religious exercise of faith and, as such, it had no secular purpose.

We the People, Copyright © Pamela A. Marx

Widmar v. *Vincent*, 454 U.S. 263 (1981). A state-run university excluded religious groups from using its facilities, even though they were open for use by other student groups. The Court held that when a state-run university creates a forum for students to speak and be heard, it may not exclude a group just because it wants to use the facilities for religious discussion and worship, unless the university can show that the restriction is necessary to further a compelling state interest. The Court applied this reasoning in *Board of Education* v. *Mergens*, 496 U.S. 226 (1990) to require a high school to allow a Christian club to meet, since the school allowed other noncurricular groups to meet.

Wisconsin v. *Yoder*, 406 U.S. 205 (1972). The Yoders, Amish parents, refused to send their children to public school beyond the eighth grade. In so refusing, they violated a Wisconsin law requiring school attendance until age 16. The Court stated that parents' interests in the religious upbringing of their children has a high value in our society. The agricultural, non-technological way of life of Amish people is an essential part of their religious beliefs and practices. Elementary education did not seriously affect those beliefs, but secondary education would. On balance, the state's interest in requiring two more years of education was minimal compared to the negative impact continued public education would have on the Yoders' religious beliefs.

A Guide to Cited Cases

Text of the Constitution

PREAMBLE

We the people of the United States, in order to form a more perfect union, establish justice, insure domestic tranquillity, provide for the common defense, promote the general welfare, and secure the blessings of liberty to ourselves and our posterity, do ordain and establish this Constitution for the United States of America.

ARTICLE I. LEGISLATIVE DEPARTMENT

Section I. Congress

All legislative powers herein granted shall be vested in a Congress of the United States, which shall consist of a Senate and a House of Representatives.

Section II. House of Representatives

1. The House of Representatives shall be composed of members chosen every second year by the people of the several States, and the electors in each State shall have the qualifications requisite for electors of the most numerous branch of the State Legislature.

2. No person shall be a Representative who shall not have attained to the age of twenty-five years, and been seven years a citizen of the United States, and who shall not, when elected, be an inhabitant of that State in which he shall be chosen.

3. Representatives *and direct taxes* shall be apportioned among the several States which may be included within this Union, according to their respective numbers, *which shall be determined by adding to the whole number of free persons, including those bound to service for a term of years, and excluding Indians not taxed, three-fifths of all other persons.* The actual enumeration shall be made within three years after the first meeting of the Congress of the United States, and within every subsequent term of ten years, in such manner as they shall by law direct. The number of Representatives shall not exceed one for every thirty thousand, but each State shall have at least one Representative; and until such enumeration shall be made, the State of New Hampshire shall be entitled to choose three, Massachusetts eight, Rhode Island and Providence Plantations one, Connecticut five, New York six, New Jersey four, Pennsylvania eight, Delaware one, Maryland six, Virginia ten, North Carolina five, South Carolina five, and Georgia three.

We the People, Copyright © Pamela A. Marx

4. When vacancies happen in the representation from any State, the Executive authority thereof shall issue writs of election to fill such vacancies.

5. The House of Representatives shall choose their Speaker and other officers; and shall have the sole power of impeachment.

Section III. Senate

1. The Senate of the United States shall be composed of two Senators from each State, *chosen by the legislature thereof,* for six years; and each Senator shall have one vote.

2. Immediately after they shall be assembled in consequence of the first election, they shall be divided as equally as may be into three classes. The seats of the Senators of the first class shall be vacated at the expiration of the second year, of the second class at the expiration of the fourth year, and of the third class at the expiration of the sixth year, so that one-third may be chosen every second year; *and if vacancies happen by resignation or otherwise, during the recess of the legislature of any State, the Executive thereof may make temporary appointments until the next meeting of the legislature, which shall then fill such vacancies.*

3. No person shall be a Senator who shall not have attained to the age of thirty years, and been nine years a citizen of the United States, and who shall not, when elected, be an inhabitant of that State for which he shall be chosen.

4. The Vice-President of the United States shall be President of the Senate, but shall have no vote, unless they be equally divided.

5. The Senate shall choose their other officers, and also a President pro tempore, in the absence of the Vice-President, or when he shall exercise the office of President of the United States.

6. The Senate shall have the sole power to try all impeachments. When sitting for that purpose, they shall be on oath or affirmation. When the President of the United States is tried, the Chief Justice shall preside: and no person shall be convicted without the concurrence of two-thirds of the members present.

7. Judgment in cases of impeachment shall not extend further than to removal from office, and disqualification to hold and enjoy any office of honor, trust or profit under the United States: but the party convicted shall nevertheless be liable and subject to indictment, trial, judgment and punishment, according to law.

Section IV. Elections and Meetings of Congress

1. The times, places and manner of holding elections for Senators and Representatives shall be prescribed in each State by the legislature thereof; but the Congress may at any time by law make or alter such regulations, except as to the places of choosing Senators.

2. The Congress shall assemble at least once in every year, and such meeting *shall be on the first Monday in December, unless they shall by law appoint a different day.*

Section V. Organization and Rules of the Houses

1. Each house shall be the judge of the elections, returns and qualifications of its own members, and a majority of each shall constitute a quorum to do business; but a smaller number may adjourn from day to day, and may be authorized to compel the attendance of absent members, in such manner, and under such penalties, as each house may provide.

2. Each house may determine the rules of its proceedings, punish its members for disorderly behavior, and with the concurrence of two-thirds, expel a member.

3. Each house shall keep a journal of its proceedings, and from time to time publish the same, excepting such parts as may in their judgment require secrecy; and the yeas and nays of the members of either house on any question shall, at the desire of one-fifth of those present, be entered on the journal.

4. Neither house, during the session of Congress, shall, without the consent of the other, adjourn for more than three days, nor to any other place than that in which the two houses shall be sitting.

Section VI. Privileges of and Prohibitions Upon Those in Congress

1. *The Senators and Representatives shall receive a compensation for their services*, to be ascertained by law and paid out of the treasury of the United States. They shall in all cases except treason, felony and breach of the peace, be privileged from arrest during their attendance at the session of their respective houses, and in going to and returning from the same; and for any speech or debate in either house, they shall not be questioned in any other place.

2. No Senator or Representative shall, during the time for which he was elected, be appointed to any civil office under the authority of the United States, which shall have been created, or the emoluments whereof shall have been increased, during such time; and no person holding any office under the United States shall be a member of either house during his continuance in office.

Section VII. The Making of Laws

1. All bills for raising revenue shall originate in the House of Representatives; but the Senate may propose or concur with amendments as on other bills.

2. Every bill which shall have passed the House of Representatives and the Senate, shall, before it become a law, be presented to the President of the United States; if he approve he shall sign it, but if not he shall return it with his objections to that house in which it shall have originated, who shall enter the objections at large on their journal, and proceed to reconsider it. If after such reconsideration two-thirds of that house shall agree to pass the bill, it shall be sent, together with the objections, to the other house, by which it shall likewise be reconsidered, and, if approved by two-thirds of that house, it shall become a law. But in all such cases the votes of both houses shall be determined by yeas and nays, and the names of the persons voting for and against the bill shall be entered on the journal of each house respectively. If any bill shall not be returned by the President within ten days (Sundays excepted) after it shall have been presented to him, the same shall be a law, in like manner as if he had signed it,

unless the Congress by their adjournment prevent its return, in which case it shall not be a law.

3. Every order, resolution, or vote to which the concurrence of the Senate and House of Representatives may be necessary (except on a question of adjournment) shall be presented to the President of the United States; and before the same shall take effect, shall be approved by him, or being disapproved by him, shall be repassed by two-thirds of the Senate and House of Representatives, according to the rules and limitations prescribed in the case of a bill.

Section VIII. Powers Granted to Congress

1. The Congress shall have power to lay and collect taxes, duties, imposts, and excises, to pay the debts and provide for the common defense and general welfare of the United States; but all duties, imposts and excises shall be uniform throughout the United States;

2. To borrow money on the credit of the United States;

3. To regulate commerce with foreign nations, and among the several States, and with the Indian tribes;

4. To establish an uniform rule of naturalization, and uniform laws on the subject of bankruptcies throughout the United States;

5. To coin money, regulate the value thereof, and of foreign coin, and fix the standard of weights and measures;

6. To provide for the punishment of counterfeiting the securities and current coin of the United States;

7. To establish post offices and post roads;

8. To promote the progress of science and useful arts by securing for limited times to authors and inventors the exclusive right to their respective writings and discoveries;

9. To constitute tribunals inferior to the Supreme Court;

10. To define and punish piracies and felonies committed on the high seas and offenses against the law of nations;

11. To declare war, grant letters of marque and reprisal, and make rules concerning captures on land and water;

12. To raise and support armies, but no appropriation of money to that use shall be for a longer term than two years;

13. To provide and maintain a navy;

14. To make rules for the government and regulation of the land and naval forces;

15. To provide for calling forth the militia to execute the laws of the Union, suppress insurrections, and repel invasions;

16. To provide for organizing, arming, and disciplining the militia, and for governing such part of them as may be employed in the service of the United States, reserving to the States respectively the appointment of the officers, and the authority of training the militia according to the discipline prescribed by Congress;

17. To exercise exclusive legislation in all cases whatsoever, over such district (not exceeding ten miles square) as may, by cession of particular States, and the acceptance of Congress, become the seat of government of the United States, and to exercise like authority over all places purchased by the consent of the legislature of the State, in which the same shall be, for the erection of forts, magazines, arsenals, dock-yards, and other needful buildings;—and

18. To make all laws which shall be necessary and proper for carrying into execution the foregoing powers, and all other powers vested by this Constitution in the government of the United States, or in any department or officer thereof.

Section IX. Powers Denied to the Federal Government

1. The migration or importation of such persons as any of the States now existing shall think proper to admit shall not be prohibited by the Congress prior to the year 1808; but a tax or duty may be imposed on such importation, not exceeding $10 for each person.

2. The privilege of the writ of habeas corpus shall not be suspended, unless when in cases of rebellion or invasion the public safety may require it.

3. No bill of attainder or ex post facto law shall be passed.

4. *No capitation, or other direct, tax shall be laid, unless in proportion to the census or enumeration herein before directed to be taken.*

5. No tax or duty shall be laid on articles exported from any State.

6. No preference shall be given by any regulation of commerce or revenue to the ports of one State over those of another; nor shall vessels bound to, or from, one State, be obliged to enter, clear, or pay duties in another.

7. No money shall be drawn from the treasury, but in consequence of appropriations made by law; and a regular statement and account of the receipts and expenditures of all public money shall be published from time to time.

8. No title of nobility shall be granted by the United States: and no person holding any office of profit or trust under them, shall, without the consent of the Congress, accept of any present, emolument, office, or title, of any kind whatever, from any king, prince, or foreign state.

Section X. Powers Denied to the States

1. No State shall enter into any treaty, alliance, or confederation; grant letters of marque and reprisal; coin money; emit bills of credit; make anything but gold and silver coin a tender in payment of debts; pass any bill of attainder, ex post facto, or law impairing the obligation of contracts, or grant any title of nobility.

2. No State shall, without the consent of the Congress, lay any imposts or duties on imports or exports, except what may be absolutely necessary for executing its inspection laws: and the net produce of all duties and imposts, laid by any State on imports or exports, shall be for the use of the treasury of the United States; and all such laws shall be subject to the revision and control of the Congress.

3. No State shall, without the consent of Congress, lay any duty of tonnage, keep troops or ships of war in time of peace, enter into any agreement or compact with another State, or with a foreign power, or engage in war, unless actually invaded, or in such imminent danger as will not admit of delay.

ARTICLE II. EXECUTIVE DEPARTMENT

Section I. President and Vice-President

1. The executive power shall be vested in a President of the United States of America. He shall hold his office during the term of four years, and, together with the Vice-President, chosen for the same term, be elected as follows:

2. Each State shall appoint, in such manner as the legislature thereof may direct, a number of electors, equal to the whole number of Senators and Representatives to which the State may be entitled in the Congress; but no Senator or Representative, or person holding an office of trust or profit under the United States, shall be appointed an elector.

The electors shall meet in their respective States, and vote by ballot for two persons, of whom one at least shall not be an inhabitant of the same State with themselves. And they shall make a list of all the persons voted for, and of the number of votes for each; which list they shall sign and certify, and transmit sealed to the seat of government of the United States, directed to the President of the Senate. The President of the Senate shall, in the presence of the Senate and the House of Representatives, open all the certificates, and the votes shall then be counted. The person having the greatest number of votes shall be the President, if such number be a majority of the whole number of electors appointed; and, if there be more than one who have such majority, and have an equal number of votes, then the House of Representatives shall immediately choose by ballot one of them for President; and if no person have a majority, then from the five highest on the list the said house shall in like manner choose the President. But in choosing the President the votes shall be taken by States, the representation from each State having one vote; a quorum for this purpose shall consist of a member or members from two-thirds of the States, and a majority of all the States shall be necessary to a choice. In every case, after the choice of the President, the person having the greatest number of votes of the electors shall be the Vice-President. But if there should remain two or more who have equal votes, the Senate shall choose from them by ballot the Vice-President.

3. The Congress may determine the time of choosing the electors and the day on which they shall give their votes; which day shall be the same throughout the United States.

4. No person except a natural-born citizen, or a citizen of the United States at the time of the adoption of this Constitution, shall be eligible to the office of President; neither shall any person be eligible to that office who shall not have attained to the age of thirty-five years, and been fourteen years a resident within the United States.

5. *In case of the removal of the President from office or of his death, resignation, or inability to discharge the powers and duties of the said office, the same shall devolve on the Vice-President, and the Congress may by law provide for the case of removal, death, resignation, or inability, both of the President and Vice-President, declaring what officer shall then act as President, and such officer shall act accordingly, until the disability be removed, or a President shall be elected.*

6. The President shall, at stated times, receive for his services a compensation, which shall neither be increased nor diminished during the period for which he shall have been elected, and he shall not receive within that period any other emolument from the United States, or any of them.

7. Before he enter on the execution of his office, he shall take the following oath or affirmation:—"I do solemnly swear (or affirm) that I will faithfully execute the office of the President of the United States, and will to the best of my ability preserve, protect and defend the Constitution of the United States."

Section II. Powers of the President

1. The President shall be commander in chief of the army and navy of the United States, and of the militia of the several States, when called into the actual service of the United States; he may require the opinion, in writing, of the principal officer in each of the executive departments, upon any subject relating to the duties of their respective offices, and he shall have power to grant reprieves and pardons for offenses against the United States, except in cases of impeachment.

2. He shall have power, by and with the advice and consent of the Senate, to make treaties, provided two-thirds of the Senators present concur; and he shall nominate, and by and with the advice and consent of the Senate, shall appoint ambassadors, other public ministers and consuls, judges of the Supreme Court, and all other officers of the United States, whose appointments are not herein otherwise provided for, and which shall be established by law: but the Congress may by law vest the appointment of such inferior officers, as they think proper, in the President alone, in the courts of law, or in the heads of departments.

3. The President shall have power to fill up all vacancies that may happen during the recess of the Senate, by granting commissions which shall expire at the end of their next session.

Section III. Other Powers and Duties of the President

He shall from time to time give to the Congress information of the state of the Union, and recommend to their consideration such measures as he shall judge necessary and expedient; he may, on extraordinary occasions, convene both houses, or either of them, and in case of disagreement between them, with respect to the time of adjournment, he may adjourn them to such time as he shall think proper; he shall receive ambassadors and other public ministers; he shall take care that the laws be faithfully executed, and shall commission all the officers of the United States.

Section IV. Impeachment

The President, Vice-President and all civil officers of the United States shall be removed from office on impeachment for, and on conviction of, treason, bribery, and other high crimes and misdemeanors.

ARTICLE III. JUDICIAL DEPARTMENT

Section I. The Federal Court System

The judicial power of the United States shall be vested in one Supreme Court, and in such inferior courts as the Congress may from time to time ordain and establish. The judges, both of the Supreme and inferior courts, shall hold their offices during good behavior, and shall, at stated times, receive for their services a compensation which shall not be diminished during their continuance in office.

Section II. Jurisdiction of Federal Courts

1. The judicial power shall extend to all cases, in law and equity, arising under this Constitution, the laws of the United States, and treaties made, or which shall be made, under their authority;—to all cases affecting ambassadors, other public ministers and consuls;—to all cases of admiralty and maritime jurisdiction;—to controversies to which the United States shall be a party;—to controversies between two or more States;— *between a State and citizens of another State;*—between citizens of different States;— between citizens of the same State claiming lands under grants of different States, and between a State, or the citizens thereof, and foreign states, citizens or subjects.

2. In all cases affecting ambassadors, other public ministers and consuls, and those in which a State shall be party, the Supreme Court shall have original jurisdiction. In all other cases before mentioned, the Supreme Court shall have appellate jurisdiction, both as to law and fact, with such exceptions, and under such regulations, as the Congress shall make.

3. The trial of all crimes, except in cases of impeachment, shall be by jury; and such trial shall be held in the State where the said crimes shall have been committed; but when not committed within any State, the trial shall be at such place or places as the Congress may by law have directed.

Section III. Treason

1. Treason against the United States shall consist only in levying war against them, or in adhering to their enemies, giving them aid and comfort. No person shall be convicted of treason unless on the testimony of two witnesses to the same overt act, or on confession in open court.

2. The Congress shall have power to declare the punishment of treason, but no attainder of treason shall work corruption of blood, or forfeiture except during the life of the person attainted.

ARTICLE IV. HOW THE STATES RELATE TO ONE ANOTHER

Section I. Honoring of Acts, Records, and Court Decisions of the States

Full faith and credit shall be given in each State to the public acts, records, and judicial proceedings of every other State. And the Congress may by general laws prescribe the manner in which such acts, records, and proceedings shall be proved, and the effect thereof.

Section II. Duties of States to Each Other

1. The citizens of each State shall be entitled to all privileges and immunities of citizens in the several States.

2. A person charged in any State with treason, felony, or other crime, who shall flee from justice, and be found in another State, shall on demand of the executive authority of the State from which he fled, be delivered up, to be removed to the State having jurisdiction of the crime.

3. *No person held to service or labor in one State, under the laws thereof, escaping into another, shall, in consequence of any law or regulation therein, be discharged from such service or labor, but shall be delivered up on claim of the party to whom such service or labor may be due.*

Section III. New States and Territories

1. New States may be admitted by the Congress into this Union; but no new State shall be formed or erected within the jurisdiction of any other State; nor any State be formed by the junction of two or more States, or parts of States, without the consent of the legislatures of the States concerned as well as of the Congress.

2. The Congress shall have power to dispose of and make all needful rules and regulations respecting the territory or other property belonging to the United States; and nothing in this Constitution shall be so construed as to prejudice any claims of the United States, or of any particular State.

Section IV. Federal Protection Guaranteed to the States

The United States shall guarantee to every State in this Union a republican form of government, and shall protect each of them against invasion; and on application of the legislature, or of the executive (when the legislature cannot be convened), against domestic violence.

ARTICLE V. AMENDING THE CONSTITUTION

The Congress, whenever two-thirds of both houses shall deem it necessary, shall propose amendments to this Constitution, or, on the application of the legislatures of two-thirds of the several States, shall call a convention for proposing amendments, which, in either case, shall be valid to all intents and purposes, as part of this Constitution, when ratified by the legislatures of three-fourths of the several States, or by conventions in three-fourths thereof, as the one or the other mode of ratification may be proposed by the Congress; provided that no amendments which may be made prior to the year one thousand eight hundred and eight shall in any manner affect the first and fourth clauses in the ninth section of the first article; and that no State, without its consent, shall be deprived of its equal suffrage in the Senate.

ARTICLE VI. GENERAL PROVISIONS

1. All debts contracted and engagements entered into, before the adoption of this Constitution, shall be as valid against the United States under this Constitution, as under the Confederation.

2. This Constitution, and the laws of the United States which shall be made in pursuance thereof; and all treaties made, or which shall be made, under the authority of the United States, shall be the supreme law of the land; and the judges in every State shall be bound thereby, anything in the Constitution or laws of any State to the contrary notwithstanding.

3. The Senators and Representatives before mentioned, and the members of the several State legislatures, and all executive and judicial officers, both of the United States and of the several States, shall be bound by oath or affirmation to support this Constitution; but no religious test shall ever be required as a qualification to any office or public trust under the United States.

ARTICLE VII. RATIFICATION OF THE CONSTITUTION

The ratification of the conventions of nine States shall be sufficient for the establishment of this Constitution between the States so ratifying the same.

Done in Convention by the unanimous consent of the States present, the seventeenth day of September in the year of our Lord one thousand seven hundred and eighty-seven and of the Independence of the United States of America the twelfth. In witness whereof we have hereunto subscribed our names.

[George Washington as President and Deputy from Virginia and 38 others signed.]

AMENDMENTS TO THE CONSTITUTION

Amendment I. Religious and Political Freedom

Congress shall make no law respecting an establishment of religion, or prohibiting the free exercise thereof; or abridging the freedom of speech, or of the press; or the right of the people peaceably to assemble, and to petition the government for a redress of grievances.

Amendment II. Right to Bear Arms

A well-regulated militia being necessary to the security of a free State, the right of the people to keep and bear arms shall not be infringed.

Amendment III. Quartering of Troops

No soldier shall, in time of peace, be quartered in any house without the consent of the owner, nor in time of war, but in a manner to be prescribed by law.

Amendment IV. Search And Seizure

The right of the people to be secure in their persons, houses, papers, and effects, against unreasonable searches and seizures, shall not be violated, and no warrants shall issue but upon probable cause, supported by oath or affirmation, and particularly describing the place to be searched, and the persons or things to be seized.

Amendment V. No Self-Incrimination and Right to Life, Liberty, and Property

No person shall be held to answer for a capital, or otherwise infamous crime, unless on a presentment or indictment of a grand jury, except in cases arising in the land or naval forces, or in the militia, when in actual service in time of war or public danger; nor shall any person be subject for the same offense to be twice put in jeopardy of life or limb; nor shall be compelled in any criminal case to be a witness against himself, nor be deprived of life, liberty, or property, without due process of law; nor shall private property be taken for public use without just compensation.

Amendment VI. Criminal Trial Protections

In all criminal prosecutions, the accused shall enjoy the right to a speedy and public trial, by an impartial jury of the State and district wherein the crime shall have been committed, which district shall have been previously ascertained by law, and to be informed of the nature and cause of the accusation; to be confronted with the witnesses against him; to have compulsory process for obtaining witnesses in his favor, and to have the assistance of counsel for his defense.

Amendment VII. Noncriminal Cases

In suits at common law, where the value in controversy shall exceed twenty dollars, the right of trial by jury shall be preserved, and no fact tried by a jury shall be otherwise re-examined in any court of the United States, than according to the rules of the common law.

Amendment VIII. Bail and Punishments

Excessive bail shall not be required, nor excessive fines imposed, nor cruel and unusual punishments inflicted.

Amendment IX. About Rights Not Listed

The enumeration in the Constitution, of certain rights, shall not be construed to deny or disparage others retained by the people.

Amendment X. Powers Reserved to the States and to the People

The powers not delegated to the United States by the Constitution, nor prohibited by it to the States, are reserved to the States respectively, or to the people.

Amendment XI. Limit on Federal Court Jurisdiction

The judicial power of the United States shall not be construed to extend to any suit in law or equity, commenced or prosecuted against one of the United States by citizens of another State, or by citizens or subjects of any foreign state.

Amendment XII. Election of President and Vice-President

1. The electors shall meet in their respective States, and vote by ballot for President and Vice-President, one of whom, at least, shall not be an inhabitant of the same State

with themselves; they shall name in their ballots the person voted for as President, and in distinct ballots the person voted for as Vice-President, and they shall make distinct lists of all persons voted for as President, and of all persons voted for as Vice-President, and of the number of votes for each, which lists they shall sign and certify, and transmit sealed to the seat of government of the United States, directed to the President of the Senate;—the President of the Senate shall, in the presence of the Senate and House of Representatives, open all the certificates and the votes shall then be counted;—the person having the greatest number of votes for President shall be the President, if such number be a majority of the whole number of electors appointed; and if no person have such majority, then from the persons having the highest numbers not exceeding three on the list of those voted for as President, the House of Representatives shall choose immediately, by ballot, the President. But in choosing the President, the votes shall be taken by States, the representation from each State having one vote; a quorum for this purpose shall consist of a member or members from two-thirds of the States, and a majority of all the States shall be necessary to a choice. And if the House of Representatives shall not choose a President whenever the right of choice shall devolve upon them, before *the fourth day of March* next following, then the Vice-President shall act as President, as in the case of the death or other constitutional disability of the President.

2. The person having the greatest number of votes as Vice-President shall be the Vice-President, if such number be a majority of the whole number of electors appointed; and if no person have a majority, then from the two highest numbers on the list the Senate shall choose the Vice-President; a quorum for the purpose shall consist of two-thirds of the whole number of Senators, and a majority of the whole number shall be necessary to a choice. But no person constitutionally ineligible to the office of President shall be eligible to that of Vice-President of the United States.

Amendment XIII. Slavery Prohibited

1. Neither slavery nor involuntary servitude, except as a punishment for crime whereof the party shall have been duly convicted, shall exist within the United States, or any place subject to their jurisdiction.

2. Congress shall have power to enforce this article by appropriate legislation.

Amendment XIV. Equal Protection and Due Process

1. All persons born or naturalized in the United States, and subject to the jurisdiction thereof, are citizens of the United States and of the State wherein they reside. No State shall make or enforce any law which shall abridge the privileges or immunities of citizens of the United States; nor shall any State deprive any person of life, liberty, or property, without due process of law; nor deny to any person within its jurisdiction the equal protection of the laws.

2. Representatives shall be apportioned among the several States according to their respective numbers, counting the whole number of persons in each State, excluding Indians not taxed. But when the right to vote at any election for the choice of electors for President and Vice-President of the United States, Representatives in Congress, the executive and judicial officers of a State, or the members of the legislature there-

of, is denied to any of the male inhabitants of such State, being twenty-one years of age and citizens of the United States, or in any way abridged, except for participation in rebellion, or other crime, the basis of representation therein shall be reduced in the proportion which the number of such male citizens shall bear to the whole number of male citizens twenty-one years of age in such State.

3. No person shall be a Senator or Representative in Congress, or Elector of President and Vice-President, or hold any office, civil or military, under the United States, or under any State, who, having previously taken an oath, as a member of Congress, or as an officer of the United States, or as a member of any State legislature, or as an executive or judicial officer of any State, to support the Constitution of the United States, shall have engaged in insurrection or rebellion against the same, or given aid or comfort to the enemies thereof. But Congress may, by a vote of two-thirds of each house, remove such disability.

4. The validity of the public debt of the United States, authorized by law, including debts incurred for payment of pensions and bounties for services in suppressing insurrection or rebellion, shall not be questioned. But neither the United States nor any State shall assume or pay any debt or obligation incurred in aid of insurrection or rebellion against the United States, or any claim for the loss or emancipation of any slave; but all such debts, obligations, and claims shall be held illegal and void.

5. The Congress shall have power to enforce, by appropriate legislation, the provisions of this article.

Amendment XV. No Denial of Voting Rights Based on Race, Etc.

1. The right of citizens of the United States to vote shall not be denied or abridged by the United States or by any State on account of race, color, or previous condition of servitude.

2. The Congress shall have power to enforce this article by appropriate legislation.

Amendment XVI. Income Taxes

The Congress shall have power to lay and collect taxes on incomes, from whatever source derived, without apportionment among the several States, and without regard to any census or enumeration.

Amendment XVII. Direct Election of Senators

1. The Senate of the United States shall be composed of two Senators from each State, elected by the people thereof, for six years; and each Senator shall have one vote. The electors in each State shall have the qualifications requisite for electors of the most numerous branch of the State legislatures.

2. When vacancies happen in the representation of any State in the Senate, the executive authority of such State shall issue writs of election to fill such vacancies: Provided, that the Legislature of any State may empower the executive thereof to make temporary appointments until the people fill the vacancies by election as the Legislature may direct.

3. This amendment shall not be so construed as to affect the election or term of any Senator chosen before it becomes valid as part of the Constitution.

Amendment XVIII. Prohibition

1. *After one year from the ratification of this article the manufacture, sale, or transportation of intoxicating liquors within, the importation thereof into, or the exportation thereof from the United States and all territory subject to the jurisdiction thereof, for beverage purposes, is hereby prohibited.*

2. *The Congress and the several States shall have concurrent power to enforce this article by appropriate legislation.*

3. *This article shall be inoperative unless it shall have been ratified as an amendment to the Constitution by the legislatures of the several States, as provided by the Constitution, within seven years from the date of the submission thereof to the States by the Congress.*

Amendment XIX. Voting Rights for Women

1. The right of citizens of the United States to vote shall not be denied or abridged by the United States or by any State on account of sex.

2. The Congress shall have power to enforce this article by appropriate legislation.

Amendment XX. Presidential and Congressional Terms

1. The terms of the President and Vice-President shall end at noon on the 20th day of January, and the terms of Senators and Representatives at noon on the 3d day of January, of the years in which such terms would have ended if this article had not been ratified; and the terms of their successors shall then begin.

2. The Congress shall assemble at least once in every year, and such meeting shall begin at noon on the 3d day of January, unless they shall by law appoint a different day.

3. If, at the time fixed for the beginning of the term of the President, the President-elect shall have died, the Vice-President-elect shall become President. If a President shall not have been chosen before the time fixed for beginning of his term, or if the President-elect shall have failed to qualify, then the Vice-President-elect shall act as President until a President shall have qualified; and the Congress may by law provide for the case wherein neither a President-elect nor a Vice-President-elect shall have qualified, declaring who shall then act as President, or the manner in which one who is to act shall be selected, and such persons shall act accordingly until a President or Vice-President shall have qualified.

4. The Congress may by law provide for the case of the death of any of the persons from whom the House of Representatives may choose a President whenever the right of choice shall have devolved upon them, and for the case of the death of any of the persons from whom the Senate may choose a Vice-President whenever the right of choice shall have devolved upon them.

5. Sections 1 and 2 shall take effect on the 15th day of October following the ratification of this article.

6. This article shall be inoperative unless it shall have been ratified as an amendment to the Constitution by the legislatures of three-fourths of the several States within seven years from the date of its submission.

Amendment XXI. Prohibition Repealed

1. The eighteenth article of amendment to the Constitution of the United States is hereby repealed.

2. The transportation or importation into any State, Territory, or Possession of the United States for delivery or use therein of intoxicating liquors, in violation of the laws thereof, is hereby prohibited.

3. This article shall be inoperative unless it shall have been ratified as an amendment to the Constitution by conventions in the several States, as provided in the Constitution, within seven years from the date of the submission thereof to the States by the Congress.

Amendment XXII. No Third Term for President

1. No person shall be elected to the office of President more than twice, and no person who has held the office of President, or acted as President, for more than two years of a term to which some other person was elected President shall be elected to the office of President more than once. But this article shall not apply to any person holding the office of President when this article was proposed by the Congress, and shall not prevent any person who may be holding the office of President, or acting as President, during the term within which this article becomes operative from holding the office of President or acting as President during the remainder of such term.

2. This article shall be inoperative unless it shall have been ratified as an amendment to the Constitution by the legislatures of three-fourths of the several States within seven years from the date of its submission to the States by the Congress.

Amendment XXIII. District of Columbia Voting Rights

1. The District constituting the seat of Government of the United States shall appoint in such manner as the Congress may direct:

A number of electors of President and Vice-President equal to the whole number of Senators and Representatives in Congress to which the District would be entitled if it were a State, but in no event more than the least populous State; they shall be in addition to those appointed by the States, but they shall be considered for the purposes of the election of President and Vice-President, to be electors appointed by a State; and they shall meet in the District and perform such duties as provided by the twelfth article of amendment.

2. The Congress shall have the power to enforce this article by appropriate legislation.

Amendment XXIV. No Denial of Voting Rights by Requiring Poll Taxes

1. The right of citizens of the United States to vote in any primary or other election for President or Vice-President, for electors for President or Vice-President, or for Senator or Representative in Congress, shall not be denied or abridged by the United

States or any State by reason of failure to pay any poll tax or other tax.

2. The Congress shall have the power to enforce this article by appropriate legislation.

Amendment XXV. Presidential Succession and Disability

1. In case of the removal of the President from office or of his death or resignation, the Vice-President shall become President.

2. Whenever there is a vacancy in the office of the Vice-President, the President shall nominate a Vice-President who shall take office upon confirmation by a majority vote of both Houses of Congress.

3. Whenever the President transmits to the President pro tempore of the Senate and the Speaker of the House of Representatives his written declaration that he is unable to discharge the powers and duties of his office, and until he transmits to them a written declaration to the contrary, such powers and duties shall be discharged by the Vice-President as Acting President.

4. Whenever the Vice-President and a majority of either the principal officers of the executive departments or of such other body as Congress may by law provide, transmit to the President pro tempore of the Senate and the Speaker of the House of Representatives their written declaration that the President is unable to discharge the powers and duties of his office, the Vice-President shall immediately assume the powers and duties of the office as Acting President.

Thereafter, when the President transmits to the President pro tempore of the Senate and the Speaker of the House of Representatives his written declaration that no inability exists, he shall resume the powers and duties of his office unless the Vice-President and a majority of either the principal officers of the executive department or of such other body as Congress may by law provide, transmit within four days to the President pro tempore of the Senate and the Speaker of the House of Representatives their written declaration that the President is unable to discharge the powers and duties of his office. Thereupon Congress shall decide the issue, assembling within forty-eight hours for that purpose if not in session. If the Congress, within twenty-one days after receipt of the latter written declaration, or, if Congress is not in session, within twenty-one days after Congress is required to assemble, determines by two-thirds vote of both Houses that the President is unable to discharge the powers and duties of his office, the Vice-President shall continue to discharge the same as Acting President; otherwise, the President shall resume the powers and duties of his office.

Amendment XXVI. Voting Age Lowered to Age 18

1. The right of citizens of the United States, who are eighteen years of age or older, to vote shall not be denied or abridged by the United States or by any State on account of age.

2. The Congress shall have power to enforce this article by appropriate legislation.

Amendment XXVII. Compensation for Those in Congress

No law varying the compensation for the services of the senators and representatives shall take effect, until an election of representatives shall have intervened.

Constitutional Resources
(includes useful American history resources)

Books

Bergheim, Laura. *The Washington Historical Atlas: Who Did What When and Where in the Nation's Capital.* Rockville, MD: Woodbine House, 1992.

Douglass, Frederick. *Life & Times of Frederick Douglass.* New York: Citadel Press, 1983.

Gulatta, Charles. *Extraordinary Women in Politics.* New York: Children's Press, 1998. (Book includes women in both American and world politics.)

Hakim, Joy. *A History of US: An Age of Extremes.* New York: Oxford University Press, 1994. (History covers late 19th and early 20th centuries.)

Lester, Julius. *To Be a Slave.* New York: Scholastic, Inc., 1968.

Lewis, Anthony. *Gideon's Trumpet.* New York: Random House, 1966.

Melzer, Milton. *The American Revolutionaries: A History in Their Own Words, 1750-1800.* New York: Harper Trophy, 1987.

Melzer, Milton. *The Black Americans: A History in Their Own Words, 1619-1983.* New York: Harper Collins, 1984. (Additional titles by Melzer are *Voices from the Civil War, The Bill of Rights: How We Got It and What It Means, Poverty in America, Crime in America,* and *American Politics: How It Really Works.)*

Ochoa, George. *Amazing Hispanic American History: A Book of Answers for Kids.* New York, John Wiley & Sons, Inc. 1998.

Pious, Richard. *The Presidency.* Englewood Cliffs, New Jersey: Silver Burdett Press, 1991.

Sullivan, George. *Campaigns and Elections.* Englewood Cliffs, New Jersey: Silver Burdett Press, 1991.

Sullivan, George. *Choosing the Candidates.* Englewood Cliffs, New Jersey: Silver Burdett Press, 1991.

Organizations

American Bar Association (Public Education Group), 750 North Lake Shore Drive, Chicago, Illinois 60611, 312-988-5735, http://www.abanet.org/publiced

Center for Constitutional Rights, 666 Broadway, New York, New York 10012, 212-614-6464
(This center publishes an annual report on constitutional litigation in which its attorneys are involved.)

Constitutional Rights Foundation, 601 South Kingsley Drive, Los Angeles, California 90005, 213-487-5590, http://www.crf-usa.org

Project Vote Smart, 129 NW Fourth Street, Suite 204, Corvallis, Oregon 97330, 888-VOTE-SMART or 541-754-2746, http://www.vote-smart.org

The Smithsonian
http://educate.si.edu

U.S. Government Printing Office, Superintendent of Documents, Mail Stop SSOP, Washington, D.C. 20402-9328, 202-512-1800 or 888-293-6498, http://www.access.gpo.gov

Research publications and Web sites

Congressional Directory, publication of the U.S. Government Printing Office

The United States Government Manual, publication of the U.S. Government Printing Office

Voter's Self-Defense Manual, publication of Project Vote Smart

Federal government information
http://thomas.loc.gov

U.S. Government Printing Office site (includes judicial documents and other government publications): http://www.access.gpo.gov

Congressional Record and other government documents

Congressional Record 1995-2000
http://www.access.gpo.gov/su_docs/aces/aces150.html

Congressional Record 1983-2000
http://www.access.gpo.gov/su_docs/aces/aaces190.html

Supreme Court opinions
http://www.findlaw.com/casecode/supreme.html

General law references
http://www.findlaw.com

Answer Key

The Preamble (p. 4)

Answers will vary.

Article I - The Legislative Branch—What Is the Legislative Branch and Who Can Serve? (p. 6)

Senator's term - six years/answers will vary; *Note: in the original Section III, Clause 2, the state legislatures chose each state's senators/* the "people" in each state now choose their senators; Section II, Clause 3 provided that each slave counted for 3/5 of a person; the 13th Amendment outlawed slavery

Article I - When Congress Is in Session, Who Takes the Lead? (p. 8)

speaker presides over the House; vice-president presides over the Senate; president pro tempore presides in the vice-president's absence

Article I - Membership in Congress—Conduct, Privileges, and Restrictions (p. 10)

the actual enumeration is made every 10 years/ called a census; last census taken as of April 1, 2000; 2/3 vote required to expel a member; the *Congressional Record*, or daily journal of the Congress, must record the proceedings of each House and, if 1/5 of those present so vote, the yea and nay votes of members on questions presented/ *Note: Article I, Section VII, Clause 2 states that all yea/nay override votes on vetoed bills must be recorded in the journal*

Article I - How Congress Makes Law (p. 12)

revenue raising bills must start in the House of Representatives/*Note: most common type of revenue raising bill is one proposing new taxes or changes in existing tax laws; a majority; Note: president signs a bill if he or she likes it and wants it to become law/ alternately, a bill becomes law even if the president does not sign it if the president fails to return it to Congress within 10 days (Sunday excepted) after it is presented to him or her/* if the president vetoes a bill, he or she must return it to the house from which it originated within 10 days together with a statement setting forth his or her objections to it/ a bill is also vetoed (pocket veto) if it is not signed and Congress adjourns before the 10 days run

Article I - Impeachment (p. 14)

the president and vice-president may be impeached for treason, bribery, and other high crimes and misdemeanors; Chief Justice of Supreme Court presides over the Senate trial that follows from impeachment of a president; *Note: vice-president presides over other trials in the Senate, except in the event of his own impeachment;* Senate must convict by a 2/3 vote to convict an impeached official; removal from office and disqualification to serve in other United States offices is punishment for conviction; after Senate conviction, a person can be subject to indictment, trial, judgment, and punishment under the law for any crimes allegedly committed

Article I - The Express Powers of the Legislative Branch (p. 16)

Clause 2 authorizes borrowing money; Clause 3 authorizes regulation of commerce between states and with foreign countries; Clause 7 authorizes establishment of post offices and post roads; Clause 8 authorizes establishment of a system of copyrights and patents

Article I - The "Elastic Clause" and the Implied Powers of Congress (p. 18)

Answers will vary.

Article I - Prohibitions on the Powers of Congress and the States (p. 20)

slave trade could not be prohibited by Congress prior to 1808; writ of habeas corpus cannot be suspended; 16th Amendment allowed Congress to lay tax on personal income

Take Another Look - In a State of Crisis (p. 21)

The constitutional sections violated were Article I, Section IX, Clause 2; Article I, Section VIII, Clause 12; and Article 1, Section IX, Clause 7, respectively.

Article II – Executive Department—Election and Term of Office (p. 22)

presidential term - 4 years; 22nd Amendment limits presidents to serving two terms; electors; 12th Amendment changed the electoral voting process

Article II - Presidential Qualifications and Vacancies (p. 24)

natural-born citizen, at least 35 years old, 14 years a resident within the United States; vice-president; Congress; president; majority vote; president pro tempore of the senate and speaker of the House of Representatives/ vice-president as acting president

Article II - The Powers of the President (p. 26)

commander in chief; in cases of impeachment; 2/3 vote of the Senate; ambassadors, consuls, Supreme Court judges

Article III - The Judicial Branch—The "What" and "Who" of the Judicial Branch (p. 28)

Supreme Court; Congress; answers will vary but may include false tax returns and perjury; compensation cannot be diminished; answers may vary but a likely one is that reduction in compensation could be used as a way to punish judges for unpopular decisions or the threat of reduction used to influence their decisions

Article III - All Kinds of Cases (p. 30)

answers may include cases arising under the Constitution, laws of the United States, and its treaties/ cases involving ambassadors/ admiralty, maritime cases/ cases in which the United States is a party/ cases between two or more states; original; appellate; criminal cases excluding impeachment/ in the state in which the crime was committed/ answers will vary; two witnesses

Article III - The Power of Judicial Review (p. 32)

Section II, Clause 2 of Article III

Article IV - State to State—How the States Relate (p. 34)

answers will vary; that the fugitive "be delivered up, to be removed to the State having jurisdiction...."; Congress; the legislatures of the affected states and Congress; the power to dispose of and the power to make all necessary laws regarding them; a republican form of government/ protection against invasion or, when asked, against domestic violence

Articles V and VI - Amendments to the Constitution and Federal Supremacy (p. 36)

2/3 vote of both houses of Congress; 2/3; 3/4; the laws of the United States, and its treaties

Article VII - Ratification of the Constitution (p. 38)

nine; the people; to the states and to the people

The First Amendment - Freedom of Religion (p. 40)

Congress; answers will vary

Freedom of Speech (p. 42)

Answers will vary.
The three bulleted items are to stimulate classroom discussion. No specific answers are required. Some discussion guidelines are:

* Is Mary Mouth lying? She has taken an oath to tell the truth. If she had the right to say whatever she wanted in court under oath, how would our justice system be jeopardized? Has Mary Mouth perjured herself?
* Is Ted Talker orally offending anyone with his ideas? Are people free to look the other way? Does the government have the right to protect children from seeing the words Ted has on his shirt? Are those interests greater than Ted's right to express his ideas?
* Can students express their views in any other way? What are those ways? Is the protest march during lunch or nutrition break? Does it make a difference if it is during class time? Is the demonstration blocking access to buildings? Can students get to their classes? Does the principal have a right to clear the area to insure students can get to class and study in a quiet environment? Should the principal have a right to limit overt disrespect of himself and faculty? Again, do the students have other ways of expressing their ideas?

Answers will vary.

Freedom of the Press and Free Assembly (p. 44)

to limit or prevent the open and free dissemination of information; answers may vary/ for the first case, answers may indicate that information on deployment of troops should be limited by prior restraint to protect U.S. troops/ for the second case, answers should indicate that the Supreme Court found that the court's prior restraint was not acceptable because other methods of protecting fair trial are available; meetings with government officials and visiting congressional representatives, attending election time meet-the-candidate events, PTA meetings, service clubs, political party meetings, candidate forums; the right to ask the government to correct a problem or to otherwise compensate you for losses or injury as a result of problems

The Second and Third Amendments - The Right to Bear Arms and More (p. 46)

definitions will vary; a well-regulated state militia such as the national guard is necessary to the security of a free state; answers will vary; answers will vary; can be done in peacetime only with consent of owner

The Fourth Amendment - Searches, Seizures, and Probable Cause (p. 48)

probable cause; particular description of the place to be searched and the people and/or things to be seized; answers will vary

The Fifth Amendment - Double Jeopardy, Self-Incrimination, and More (p. 50)

answers will vary but should describe crimes allowing for death as one of the punishments upon conviction; indictment by a grand jury; "to be twice put in jeopardy of life or limb"; the person refuses to be a witness against him or herself; answers will vary

The Sixth Amendment - Our Rights in a Criminal Trial (p. 52)

speedy trial preserves the freshness of evidence and availability of witnesses/ public trial helps assure fair dealing with the accused because the prosecutors and judge cannot work in secret; a jury chosen from the state and local area in which the crime was committed; the charges against him and the alleged crime—"nature and cause of the accusation"; he can confront those who testify against him; witnesses in his favor; an attorney

The Seventh and Eighth Amendments - More About the Court System (p. 54)

it cannot be excessive; fines cannot be excessive; imprisonment, death penalty; cruel and unusual; jury trial

About the Author

Pamela A. Marx is an attorney who has practiced corporate law, specializing in cable television and First Amendment issues, and dependency law with an emphasis on the educational rights of disabled children. Pamela received her B.A. and J.D. from the University of Southern California and has written several books for teachers on a variety of subjects.